As a Man Thinketh
X
Out from the Heart

James Allen

HEATHEN EDITIONS
THEIR BOOKS. OUR WAY.

Published in the good ole United States of America
by Heathen Editions, an imprint of
Heathen Creative
P.O. Box 588
Point Pleasant, WV 25550-0588

Heathen Editions are available at quantity discounts.
Bear witness to the yackety-yak and tomfoolery at:

heatheneditions.com

Social? Tag us! @heatheneditions
Photo? Tag it! #heathenedition

Caution: This book may alter your mind.

As a Man Thinketh first published July 1903
Out from the Heart first published February 1904
Heathen Edition published June 5, 2025

Paperback ISBN: 978-1-948316-40-8
Hardcover ISBN: 978-1-963228-40-3

Heathen logo, colophon, design, Heathenry, and footnotes
Copyright © Heathen Creative, LLC 2025

All rights reserved.

Book and cover design by Sheridan Cleland
Set in 11pt New Century Schoolbook
Titles in Gorilla

FIRST HEATHEN EDITION

"A wonderful little classic."
—Elizabeth R. Hogan, *The Power of Words in Your Life*

"The full impact of **As a Man Thinketh** can best be seen in the successive generations of everyday readers who embraced its aphoristic lessons directing one's thoughts to higher aims, and to understand success as the outer manifestation of inner development."
—Mitch Horowitz, *One Simple Idea*

"Years ago, I read a little book that had a lasting and profound effect on my life. It was called **As a Man Thinketh** by James Allen." —Dale Carnegie

"The reading of these books brings contentment, peace, courage, kindness, joy, and love. These strengthen the will, expand the heart, enrich the blood, stimulate digestion, and fill the being with vitality, power, and poise."
—*The Business Philosopher*

"A little book of quiet thought and sound thinking."
—*The Fort Worth Record and Register*

"Every man and woman who thinks should have a copy. It is a reasonable appeal to reasonable people who are beginning to find out that they are themselves the makers of their whole lives, by the thoughts which they continually think." —*Unity*

"One of the most stimulating and inspiring little books of all time."
—Lilian Eichler Watson, *Light From Many Lamps*

"Reasonable, sane, and clear enough in its context for the simplest mind to grasp, while brief enough for none who reads to grow weary... a book which will prove helpful to everyone who reads it, and it is one which should widely circulate and be read, not once but many times."
—*The Daily Nonpareil*

"Only by much searching and mining
are gold and diamonds obtained,
and man can find every truth
connected with his being
if he will dig deep into
the mine of his soul . . ."

Contents

As a Man Thinketh 1

Out from the Heart 43

James Allen: A Prophet of Meditation 79

Heathenry: Thoughts on the Text

As I craft this "Heathenry," there currently exists over 2500 different editions of *As a Man Thinketh* as a stand-alone title, and, by my count, nearly a dozen editions that collect *As a Man Thinketh* and *Out from the Heart* together into a single volume. However, I could be wrong, there may exist more . . . I mean, for books well over a century old, and in this epoch of on-demand printing, does anyone anywhere have a truly accurate tally of all the editions ever and currently printed? Regardless, based on the many offerings of these two titles, both past and present, what is it that makes me think we Heathens can offer anything different? Can we really do anything with these titles that hasn't been done before? Can we actually offer something new?

Yes—yes, I believe, we can—*surprisingly*.

First, though, let's talk James Allen. Who was he, exactly? Much biographical information can be found in the 1916 Murdo Carruthers article *James Allen: A Prophet of Meditation*, which we have included as an afterword, and which reads mostly as an obituary (even though it was published four years after Allen's death). It presents a sympathetic sketch of Allen's life and teachings, drawing special attention to Allen's insistence of the necessity for meditation. And since Mr. Carruthers covers those aspects of James Allen fairly well, however briefly, we won't repeat any of that info here.

Also, before we get to my thoughts, let's revisit what Allen had to say about *As a Man Thinketh* within the pages of his magazine *The Light of Reason*[1] when *Thinketh* was first published in July 1903:

> "In the pages of the present issue will be found particulars of my new book entitled, *As a Man Thinketh*. It deals with the power of thought, and particularly with the use and application of thought to happy and beautiful issues. I have tried to make the book simple, so that all can easily grasp and follow its teaching, and put into practice the methods which it advises. It shows how, in his own thought-world, each man holds the key to every condition, good or bad, that enters into his life, and that, by working patiently and intelligently upon his thoughts, he may remake his life, and transform his circumstances."[2]

Then, in the January 1904 issue, on the eve of the publication of *Out from the Heart*, Allen wrote:

> "About the 1st of February will appear a new book by the Editor entitled *Out from the Heart*.

---

[1] The spiritual magazine, later retitled *The Epoch*, that Allen began publishing in 1902.
[2] Allen, J. (1903, July). Editorial. *The Light of Reason* 4(1).

Heathenry: Thoughts on the Text

It will form a sequel to *As a Man Thinketh* . . . *As a Man Thinketh* deals with the power and application of thought in and to the practical issues of life in a broad and general way, but *Out from the Heart* will deal with details and particulars, showing how and by what practice the thoughts are to be strengthened and the mind purified, beginning with the lower steps before attempting the higher. Readers of the former book (the first edition of which is already nearly exhausted) will find in the latter complementary information and instruction, and all who are seeking the Right Path in life should not fail to secure these twin volumes."[3]

The month that *Out from the Heart* was released, Allen included this fun bit of trivia in his *Light of Reason* Editorial:

"The title originally selected was *Out of the Heart*, but just as it was about to be placed in the hands of the printer, Mr. Dimsdale Stocker's[4] booklet of poems came to hand bearing the identical title, which rendered it necessary to make some alteration, and the present title was selected."[5]

Now, my thoughts . . . This little book has become something of a passion project for me as it has been

---

[3] Allen, J. (1904, January). Editorial. *The Light of Reason* 5(1).
[4] Richard Dimsdale Stocker (1877–1935) was an English author, lecturer, and significant figure in the 20th century Ethical movement.
[5] Allen, J. (1904, February). Editorial. *The Light of Reason* 5(2).

ends p. xiii

shuffled in and out of our publishing queue several times since we first launched in December 2017.

I initially began work on it in January 2018, which means it was one of the first books I worked on after we published Heathen Edition #1: *The King in Yellow* and decided to keep doing this Heathen-thing, but I could never work out an exactly right combination of art and fonts that pleased me, so I'd tinker and tinker and tinker, then scrap all of my work and start over.

What you now hold in your hands is the third major inside-out revamp of this book, and definitely maybe the 928,675,412,304th version of the dotted map line on the cover. Then, I certainly complicated matters by having what I thought was the "genius idea" to work that dotted map line throughout the entire book, but only because that's what the two books when presented together feel like: a treasure quest, underscored by a notion from Allen in *As a Man Thinketh*:

> "Only by much searching and mining are gold and diamonds obtained, and man can find every truth connected with his being if he will dig deep into the mine of his soul . . ."

It was on my third reading of the text that the treasure map idea came to me as I thought about the relation of the two book titles as looping puzzle pieces of instruction: we must "thinketh," but we must do so from the heart, but not from the heart alone because thought begins in the mind, but all kinds of craziness happens up there in the mind, so those thoughts must be tempered, moderated, refined, improved, made loving by flowing "out from the heart" so that the location of the treasure

Heathenry: Thoughts on the Text

of self-improvement that we seek truly lies somewhere between the brain and the heart—somewhere between thought and love—and **X** marks that spot.

(See it, now, on the cover?)

And this notion was very much on my mind as I recently found myself, while steeped in Heathen research, suddenly learning about the *cardiocentric hypothesis*, the supposition that the heart is the primary location of human emotions, cognition, and awareness, which is a belief that can be traced back to the ancient Egyptians and Greeks. The great Aristotle[6] even contributed his two cents to the idea by surmising the heart to be the center of both emotions and intellect.

However, before Aristotle, it was Pythagoras[7] who introduced the opposing *cephalocentric hypothesis* that presumes the brain to command the dominant role in controlling the body. He argued that the soul resides in the brain and is immortal.

So, who's right?

Perhaps, they both are?

(Is now a good time to invite quantum theory to join the conversation?)

Cardiocentric means heart-centered, and *cephalocentric* means brain-centered, and I believe they are both correct (in their own way), so something like *cephalocardiocentrism* captures the idea that both the

---

[6] Aristotle (384–322 BC) was a Greek philosopher and polymath regarded as one of the most influential thinkers in the history of Western thought. He was a student of Plato and tutor to Alexander the Great, and his works cover a vast range of subjects, including logic, ethics, metaphysics, politics, natural science, and physics.

[7] Pythagoras (c. 580–500 BC) was a Greek philosopher, best known for the theorem of the right-angled triangle, who sought to interpret the entire physical world in terms of numbers and founded their systematic and mystical study.

brain and heart work as equals. Alternatively, we could opt for something a bit more concise: using *neuro* for brain and *card* for heart could deliver us *neurocardism* or *cardioneurism*.

Although, seeing as Aristotle and Pythagoras were both Greek, it makes far more sense to take an ancient Greek-inspired approach—using *psyche* for the soul and mind, *cardio* for the heart, and *neural* for the brain—to render the beautiful term *psychocardioneuralism*.

So, I guess that makes me a *psychocardioneuralist*?

And that brings me back to the beginning: Can we really do anything with these titles that hasn't been done before? Can we actually offer something new?

Yes—yes, I believe, we can . . .

We can package these two titles within a graphic design so [tongue mostly but firmly planted in cheek here] original and inspired that it required a new word just to describe it: *psychocardioneuralcentric*.

Also, it probably doesn't hurt that we've modernized the text utilizing American spellings instead of Allen's original British, and we've added nearly 90 footnotes to provide clarity, context, commentary, and definitions where necessary. Based on my research, I do not believe there is another edition currently available that is *as researched* as ours—the footnotes prove it, full stop.

Finally, upon conclusion of reading this legendary self-help duo, I hope you'll join me in ~~subscribing to~~ locating the old-yet-new *psychocardioneuralism*.

Remember: **X** marks the spot.

Sheridan Cleland
Co-Heathen
May 2025

Mind is the Master power that molds and makes,
And Man is Mind, and evermore he takes
The tool of Thought, and, shaping what he wills,
Brings forth a thousand joys, a thousand ills:—
He thinks in secret, and it comes to pass:
Environment is but his looking-glass.

As a Man Thinketh

Foreword

This little volume (the result of meditation and experience) is not intended as an exhaustive treatise on the much-written-upon subject of the power of thought. It is suggestive rather than explanatory, its object being to stimulate men and women to the discovery and perception of the truth that—

"They themselves are makers of themselves."

by virtue of the thoughts, which they choose and encourage; that mind is the master-weaver, both of the inner garment of character and the outer garment of circumstance, and that, as they may have hitherto woven in ignorance and pain they may now weave in enlightenment and happiness.

James Allen
Broad Park Avenue,
Ilfracombe,
England

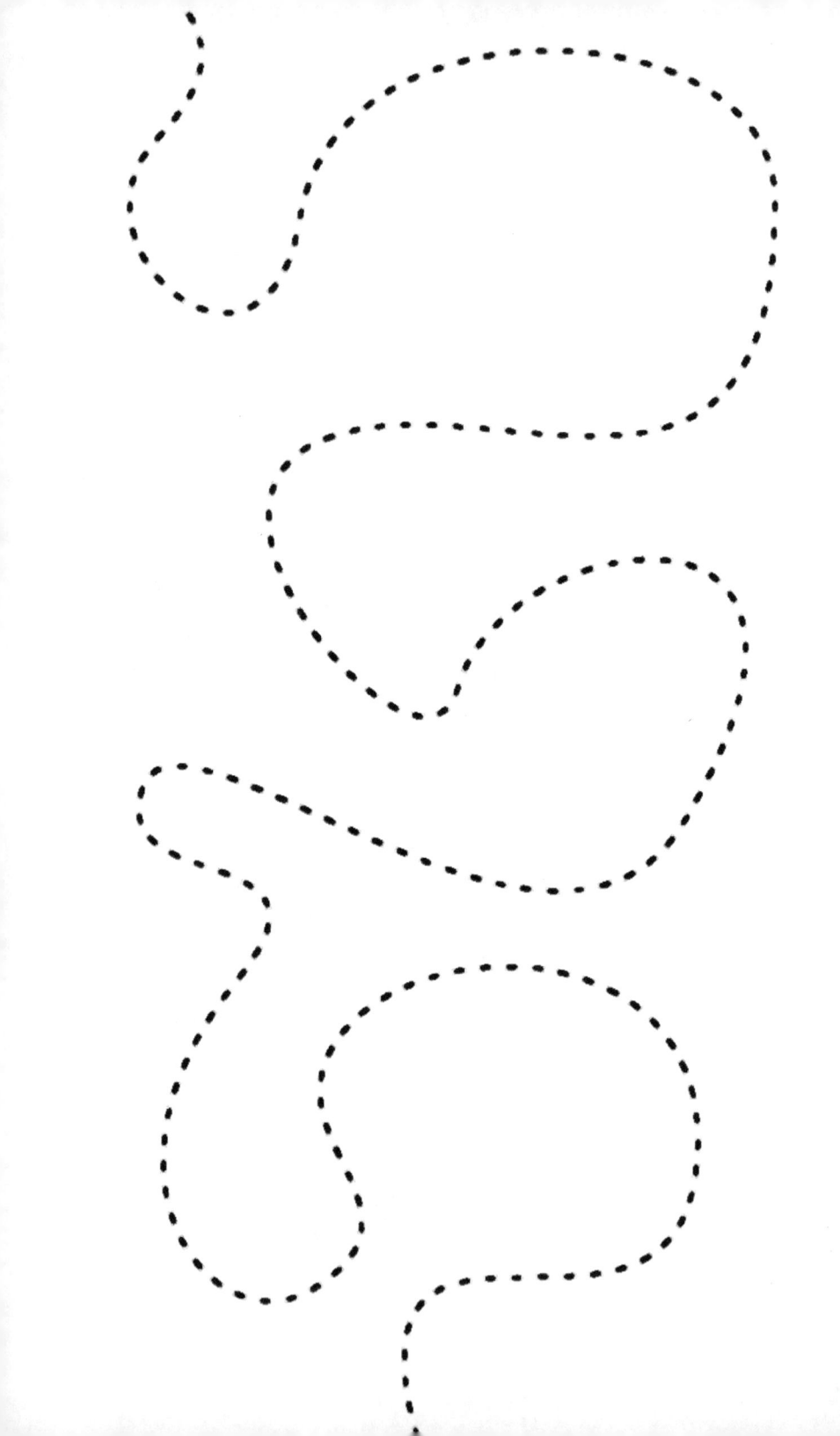

Thought & Character

The aphorism,[1] "As a man thinketh in his heart so is he," not only embraces the whole of a man's being, but is so comprehensive as to reach out to every condition and circumstance of his life. A man is literally *what he thinks*, his character being the complete sum of all his thoughts.

As the plant springs from, and could not be without, the seed, so every act of a man springs from the hidden seeds of thought, and could not have appeared without them. This applies equally to those acts called "spontaneous" and "unpremeditated" as to those which are deliberately executed.

Act is the blossom of thought, and joy and suffering are its fruits; thus does a man garner in the sweet and bitter fruitage of his own husbandry.[2]

> "Thought in the mind hath made us, What we are
> By thought was wrought and built. If a man's mind
> Hath evil thoughts, pain comes on him as comes
> The wheel the ox behind . . . .

---

[1] A statement of truth or opinion expressed in a concise manner.
[2] Farming; care and cultivation of crops and livestock.

> ... If one endure
> In purity of thought, joy follows him
> As his own shadow — sure."[3]

Man is a growth by law, and not a creation by artifice, and cause and effect is as absolute and undeviating in the hidden realm of thought as in the world of visible and material things. A noble and Godlike character is not a thing of favor or chance, but is the natural result of continued effort in right thinking, the effect of long-cherished association with Godlike thoughts. An ignoble[4] and bestial[5] character, by the same process, is the result of the continued harboring of groveling[6] thoughts.

Man is made or unmade by himself; in the armory of thought he forges the weapons by which he destroys himself; he also fashions the tools with which he builds for himself heavenly mansions of joy and strength and peace. By the right choice and true application of thought, man ascends to the Divine Perfection; by the abuse and wrong application of thought, he descends below the level of the beast. Between these two extremes are all the grades of character, and man is their maker and master.

Of all the beautiful truths pertaining to the soul which have been restored and brought to light in this age, none is more gladdening or fruitful of divine promise and confidence than this—that man is the master of thought,

---

[3] An excerpt, as translated by English poet and journalist Sir Edwin Arnold (1832–1904), from Chapter 1 of the *Dhammapada*, a collection of sayings of the Buddha in verse form and one of the most widely read and best known Buddhist scriptures. First published in Arnold's 1892 book *Potiphar's Wife and Other Poems*.

[4] Not honorable.

[5] Of or like an animal.

[6] In this context: submissive, servile, or immoral.

the molder of character, and the maker and shaper of condition, environment, and destiny.

As a being of Power, Intelligence, and Love, and the lord of his own thoughts, man holds the key to every situation, and contains within himself that transforming and regenerative agency by which he may make himself what he wills.

Man is always the master, even in his weakest and most abandoned state; but in his weakness and degradation he is the foolish master who misgoverns his "household." When he begins to reflect upon his condition, and to search diligently for the Law upon which his being is established, he then becomes the wise master, directing his energies with intelligence, and fashioning his thoughts to fruitful issues. Such is the *conscious* master, and man can only thus become by discovering *within himself* the laws of thought; which discovery is totally a matter of application, self-analysis, and experience.

Only by much searching and mining are gold and diamonds obtained, and man can find every truth connected with his being if he will dig deep into the mine of his soul; and that he is the maker of his character, the molder of his life, and the builder of his destiny, he may unerringly prove, if he will watch, control, and alter his thoughts, tracing their effects upon himself, upon others, and upon his life and circumstances, linking cause and effect by patient practice and investigation, and utilizing his every experience, even to the most trivial, everyday occurrence, as a means of obtaining that knowledge of himself which is Understanding, Wisdom, Power.

In this direction, as in no other, is the law absolute that "He that seeketh findeth; and to him that knocketh it shall be opened;"[7] for only by patience, practice, and ceaseless importunity[8] can a man enter the Door of the Temple of Knowledge.

---

[7] Matthew 7:8
[8] Persistence.

Effect of Thought on Circumstances

A man's mind may be likened to a garden, which may be intelligently cultivated or allowed to run wild; but whether cultivated or neglected, it must, and will, *bring forth*. If no useful seeds are *put* into it, then an abundance of useless weed-seeds will *fall* therein, and will continue to produce their kind.

Just as a gardener cultivates his plot, keeping it free from weeds, and growing the flowers and fruits which he requires, so may a man tend the garden of his mind, weeding out all the wrong, useless, and impure thoughts, and cultivating toward perfection the flowers and fruits of right, useful, and pure thoughts. By pursuing this process, a man sooner or later discovers that he is the master-gardener of his soul, the director of his life. He also reveals, within himself, the laws of thought, and understands, with ever-increasing accuracy, how the thought-forces and mind-elements operate in the shaping of his character, circumstances, and destiny.

Thought and character are one, and as character can only manifest and discover itself through environment and circumstance, the outer conditions of a person's life will always be found to be harmoniously related to his inner state. This does not mean that a man's circumstances at any given time are an indication of his *entire* character, but that those circumstances are so intimately connected with some vital thought-element within himself that, for the time being, they are indispensable to his development.

Every man is where he is by the law of his being; the thoughts which he has built into his character have brought him there, and in the arrangement of his life there is no element of chance, but all is the result of a law which cannot err.[1] This is just as true of those who feel "out of harmony" with their surroundings as of those who are contented with them.

As a progressive and evolving being, man is where he is that he may learn that he may grow; and as he learns the spiritual lesson which any circumstance contains for him, it passes away and gives place to other circumstances.

Man is buffeted by circumstances so long as he believes himself to be the creature of outside conditions, but when he realizes that he is a creative power, and that he may command the hidden soil and seeds of his being out of which circumstances grow, he then becomes the rightful master of himself.

That circumstances *grow* out of thought every man knows who has for any length of time practiced self-control and self-purification, for he will have noticed that the alteration in his circumstances has been in exact ratio with his altered mental condition. So true

---

[1] Be incorrect or mistaken.

Effect of Thought on Circumstances

is this that when a man earnestly applies himself to remedy the defects in his character, and makes swift and marked progress, he passes rapidly through a succession of vicissitudes.[2]

The soul attracts that which it secretly harbors; that which it loves, and also that which it fears; it reaches the height of its cherished aspirations; it falls to the level of its unchastened desires—and circumstances are the means by which the soul receives its own.

Every thought-seed sown or allowed to fall into the mind, and to take root there, produces its own, blossoming sooner or later into act, and bearing its own fruitage of opportunity and circumstance. Good thoughts bear good fruit, bad thoughts bad fruit.

The outer world of circumstance shapes itself to the inner world of thought, and both pleasant and unpleasant external conditions are factors, which make for the ultimate good of the individual. As the reaper of his own harvest, man learns both by suffering and bliss.

Following the inmost desires, aspirations, thoughts, by which he allows himself to be dominated, (pursuing the will-o'-the-wisps[3] of impure imaginings or steadfastly walking the highway of strong and high endeavor), a man at last arrives at their fruition and fulfillment in the outer conditions of his life. The laws of growth and adjustment everywhere obtain.

A man does not come to the almshouse[4] or the jail by the tyranny of fate or circumstance, but by the pathway of groveling thoughts and base desires. Nor does a pure-minded man fall suddenly into crime by stress

---

[2] Regular change from one thing to another; alternation.
[3] Things that are difficult or impossible to acquire.
[4] A house for the poor.

of any mere external force; the criminal thought had long been secretly fostered in the heart, and the hour of opportunity revealed its gathered power. Circumstance does not make the man; it reveals him to himself. No such conditions can exist as descending into vice and its attendant sufferings apart from vicious inclinations, or ascending into virtue and its pure happiness without the continued cultivation of virtuous aspirations; and man, therefore, as the lord and master of thought, is the maker of himself the shaper and author of environment. Even at birth the soul comes to its own and through every step of its earthly pilgrimage it attracts those combinations of conditions which reveal itself, which are the reflections of its own purity and impurity, its strength and weakness.

Men do not attract that which they *want*, but that which they *are*. Their whims, fancies, and ambitions are thwarted at every step, but their inmost thoughts and desires are fed with their own food, be it foul or clean. The "divinity that shapes our ends"[5] is in ourselves; it is our very self. Man is manacled[6] only by himself: thought and action are the jailers of Fate—they imprison, being base; they are also the angels of Freedom—they liberate, being noble. Not what he wishes and prays for does a man get, but what he justly earns. His wishes and prayers are only gratified and answered when they harmonize with his thoughts and actions.

In the light of this truth, what, then, is the meaning of "fighting against circumstances?" It means that a man is continually revolting against an *effect* without, while all the time he is nourishing and preserving its *cause* in

---

[5] Shakespeare's *Hamlet* (Act 5, Scene 2, Line 10).
[6] Binds; shackles; chains.

Effect of Thought on Circumstances

his heart. That cause may take the form of a conscious vice or an unconscious weakness; but whatever it is, it stubbornly retards the efforts of its possessor, and thus calls aloud for remedy.

Men are anxious to improve their circumstances, but are unwilling to improve themselves; they therefore remain bound. The man who does not shrink from self-crucifixion can never fail to accomplish the object upon which his heart is set. This is as true of earthly as of heavenly things. Even the man whose sole object is to acquire wealth must be prepared to make great personal sacrifices before he can accomplish his object; and how much more so he who would realize a strong and well-poised life?

Here is a man who is wretchedly poor. He is extremely anxious that his surroundings and home comforts should be improved, yet all the time he shirks his work, and considers he is justified in trying to deceive his employer on the ground of the insufficiency of his wages. Such a man does not understand the simplest rudiments of those principles which are the basis of true prosperity, and is not only totally unfitted to rise out of his wretchedness, but is actually attracting to himself a still deeper wretchedness by dwelling in, and acting out, indolent, deceptive, and unmanly thoughts.

Here is a rich man who is the victim of a painful and persistent disease as the result of gluttony. He is willing to give large sums of money to get rid of it, but he will not sacrifice his gluttonous desires. He wants to gratify his taste for rich and unnatural viands[7] and have his health as well. Such a man is totally unfit to have health,

[7] Food items.

because he has not yet learned the first principles of a healthy life.

Here is an employer of labor who adopts crooked measures to avoid paying the regulation wage, and, in the hope of making larger profits, reduces the wages of his work-people. Such a man is altogether unfitted for prosperity, and when he finds himself bankrupt, both as regards reputation and riches, he blames circumstances, not knowing that he is the sole author of his condition.

I have introduced these three cases merely as illustrative of the truth that man is the causer (though nearly always unconsciously) of his circumstances, and that, whilst aiming at a good end, he is continually frustrating its accomplishment by encouraging thoughts and desires which cannot possibly harmonize with that end. Such cases could be multiplied and varied almost indefinitely, but this is not necessary, as the reader can, if he so resolves, trace the action of the laws of thought in his own mind and life, and until this is done, mere external facts cannot serve as a ground of reasoning.

Circumstances, however, are so complicated, thought is so deeply rooted, and the conditions of happiness vary so vastly with individuals, that a man's *entire* soul-condition (although it may be known to himself) cannot be judged by another from the external aspect of his life alone. A man may be honest in certain directions, yet suffer privations; a man may be dishonest in certain directions, yet acquire wealth; but the conclusion usually formed that the one man fails *because of his particular honesty*, and that the other *prospers because of his particular dishonesty*, is the result of a superficial judgment, which assumes that the dishonest man is almost totally

Effect of Thought on Circumstances

corrupt, and the honest man almost entirely virtuous. In the light of a deeper knowledge and wider experience, such judgment is found to be erroneous. The dishonest man may have some admirable virtues which the other does not possess; and the honest man obnoxious vices which are absent in the other. The honest man reaps the good results of his honest thoughts and acts; he also brings upon himself the sufferings which his vices produce. The dishonest man likewise garners his own suffering and happiness.

It is pleasing to human vanity to believe that one suffers because of one's virtue; but not until a man has extirpated[8] every sickly, bitter, and impure thought from his mind, and washed every sinful stain from his soul, can he be in a position to know and declare that his sufferings are the result of his good, and not of his bad qualities; and on the way to, yet long before he has reached, that supreme perfection, he will have found, working in his mind and life, the Great Law which is absolutely just, and which cannot, therefore, give good for evil, evil for good. Possessed of such knowledge, he will then know, looking back upon his past ignorance and blindness, that his life is, and always was, justly ordered, and that all his past experiences, good and bad, were the equitable outworking of his evolving, yet unevolved self.

Good thoughts and actions can never produce bad results; bad thoughts and actions can never produce good results. This is but saying that nothing can come from corn but corn, nothing from nettles but nettles. Men understand this law in the natural world, and work with it; but few understand it in the mental and moral

---

[8] Rooted out and destroyed completely.

world (though its operation there is just as simple and undeviating), and they, therefore, do not cooperate with it.

Suffering is *always* the effect of wrong thought in some direction. It is an indication that the individual is out of harmony with himself, with the Law of his being. The sole and supreme use of suffering is to purify, to burn out all that is useless and impure. Suffering ceases for him who is pure. There could be no object in burning gold after the dross[9] had been removed, and a perfectly pure and enlightened being could not suffer.

The circumstances which a man encounters with suffering, are the result of his own mental inharmony. The circumstances which a man encounters with blessedness are the result of his own mental harmony. Blessedness, not material possessions, is the measure of right thought; wretchedness, not lack of material possessions, is the measure of wrong thought. A man may be cursed and rich; he may be blessed and poor. Blessedness and riches are only joined together when the riches are rightly and wisely used; and the poor man only descends into wretchedness when he regards his lot as a burden unjustly imposed.

Indigence[10] and indulgence are the two extremes of wretchedness. They are both equally unnatural and the result of mental disorder. A man is not rightly conditioned until he is a happy, healthy, and prosperous being; and happiness, health, and prosperity are the result of a harmonious adjustment of the inner with the outer, of the man with his surroundings.

A man only begins to be a man when he ceases to

---

[9] Rubbish.
[10] Extreme poverty.

Effect of Thought on Circumstances

whine and revile, and commences to search for the hidden justice which regulates his life. And as he adapts his mind to that regulating factor, he ceases to accuse others as the cause of his condition, and builds himself up in strong and noble thoughts; ceases to kick against circumstances, but begins to *use* them as aids to his more rapid progress, and as a means of discovering the hidden powers and possibilities within himself.

Law, not confusion, is the dominating principle in the universe; justice, not injustice, is the soul and substance of life; and righteousness, not corruption, is the molding and moving force in the spiritual government of the world. This being so, man has but to right himself to find that the universe is right; and during the process of putting himself right, he will find that as he alters his thoughts toward things and other people, things and other people will alter toward him.

The proof of this truth is in every person, and it therefore admits of easy investigation by systematic introspection and self-analysis. Let a man radically alter his thoughts, and he will be astonished at the rapid transformation it will effect in the material conditions of his life. Men imagine that thought can be kept secret, but it cannot; it rapidly crystallizes into habit, and habit solidifies into circumstance. Bestial thoughts crystallize into habits of drunkenness and sensuality, which solidify into circumstances of destitution and disease: impure thoughts of every kind crystallize into enervating[11] and confusing habits, which solidify into distracting and adverse circumstances: thoughts of fear, doubt, and indecision crystallize into weak, unmanly, and irresolute

---

[11] Energy and/or vitality draining.

habits, which solidify into circumstances of failure, indigence, and slavish dependence: lazy thoughts crystallize into habits of uncleanliness and dishonesty, which solidify into circumstances of foulness and beggary: hateful and condemnatory thoughts crystallize into habits of accusation and violence, which solidify into circumstances of injury and persecution: selfish thoughts of all kinds crystallize into habits of self-seeking, which solidify into circumstances more or less distressing. On the other hand, beautiful thoughts of all kinds crystallize into habits of grace and kindliness, which solidify into genial and sunny circumstances: pure thoughts crystallize into habits of temperance and self-control, which solidify into circumstances of repose and peace: thoughts of courage, self-reliance, and decision crystallize into manly habits, which solidify into circumstances of success, plenty, and freedom: energetic thoughts crystallize into habits of cleanliness and industry, which solidify into circumstances of pleasantness: gentle and forgiving thoughts crystallize into habits of gentleness, which solidify into protective and preservative circumstances: loving and unselfish thoughts crystallize into habits of self-forgetfulness for others, which solidify into circumstances of sure and abiding prosperity and true riches.

A particular train of thought persisted in, be it good or bad, cannot fail to produce its results on the character and circumstances. A man cannot *directly* choose his circumstances, but he can choose his thoughts, and so indirectly, yet surely, shape his circumstances.

Nature helps every man to the gratification of the thoughts which he most encourages, and opportunities

Effect of Thought on Circumstances

are presented which will most speedily bring to the surface both the good and evil thoughts.

Let a man cease from his sinful thoughts, and all the world will soften toward him, and be ready to help him; let him put away his weakly and sickly thoughts, and lo! opportunities will spring up on every hand to aid his strong resolves; let him encourage good thoughts, and no hard fate shall bind him down to wretchedness and shame. The world is your kaleidoscope, and the varying combinations of colors which at every succeeding moment it presents to you are the exquisitely adjusted pictures of your ever-moving thoughts.

"You will be what you will to be;
   Let failure find its false content
   In that poor word, 'environment,'
But spirit scorns it, and is free.

"It masters time, it conquers space;
   It cows[12] that boastful trickster, Chance,
   And bids the tyrant Circumstance
Uncrown, and fill a servant's place.

"The human Will, that force unseen,
   The offspring of a deathless Soul,
   Can hew a way to any goal,
Though walls of granite intervene.

"Be not impatient in delay,
   But wait as one who understands;
   When spirit rises and commands,
The gods are ready to obey."[13]

---

[12] Intimidates into submission.
[13] An excerpt from the poem "Will" by American author and poet Ella Wheeler Wilcox (1850–1919), first published in her 1901 collection *Poems of Power*.

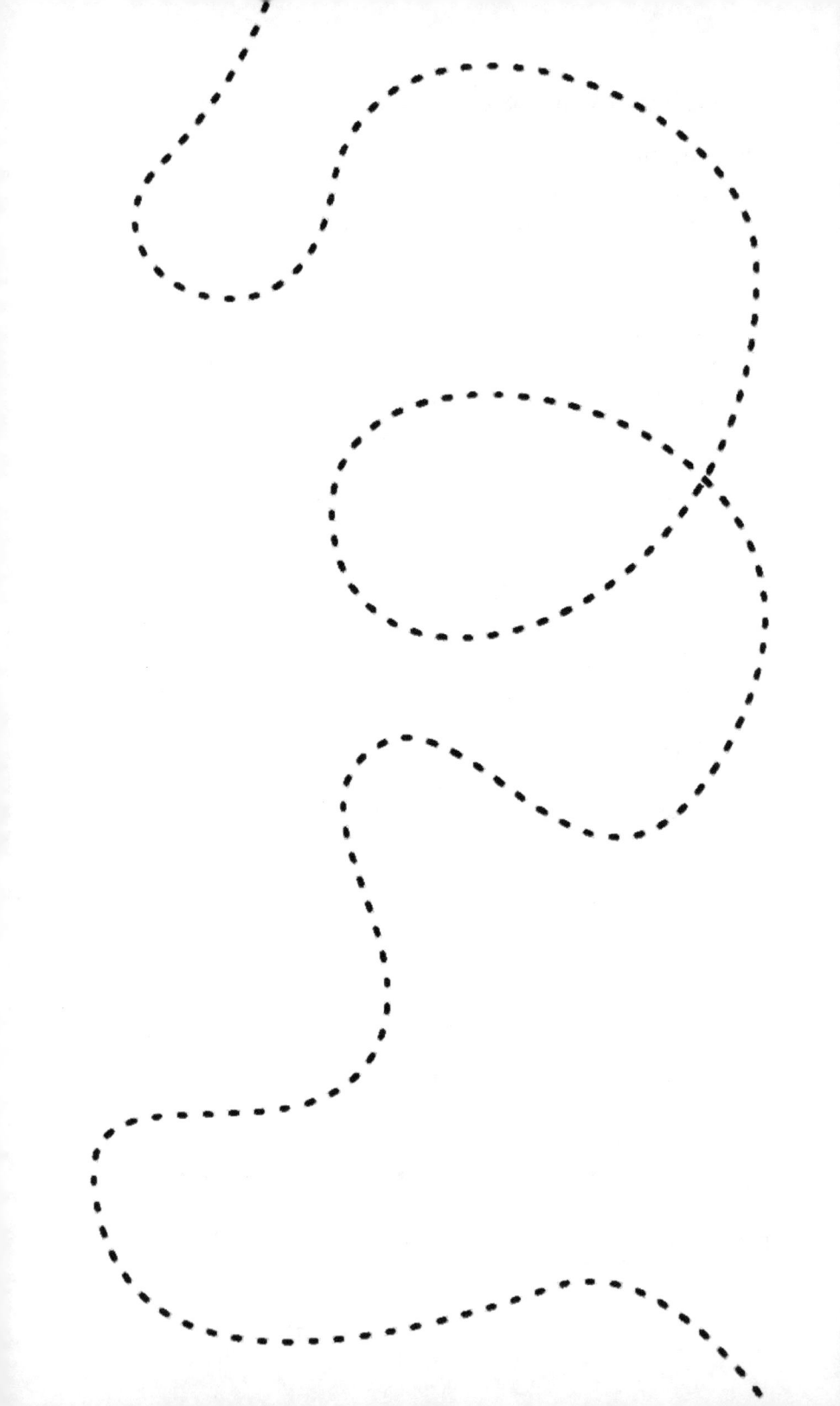

Effect of Thought on Health and the Body

The body is the servant of the mind. It obeys the operations of the mind, whether they be deliberately chosen or automatically expressed. At the bidding of unlawful thoughts the body sinks rapidly into disease and decay; at the command of glad and beautiful thoughts it becomes clothed with youthfulness and beauty.

Disease and health, like circumstances, are rooted in thought. Sickly thoughts will express themselves through a sickly body. Thoughts of fear have been known to kill a man as speedily as a bullet, and they are continually killing thousands of people just as surely though less rapidly. The people who live in fear of disease are the people who get it. Anxiety quickly demoralizes the whole body, and lays it open to the entrance of disease; while impure thoughts, even if not physically indulged, will soon shatter the nervous system.

Strong, pure, and happy thoughts build up the body in vigor and grace. The body is a delicate and plastic instrument, which responds readily to the thoughts by which it is impressed, and habits of thought will produce their own effects, good or bad, upon it.

Men will continue to have impure and poisoned blood so long as they propagate unclean thoughts. Out of a clean heart comes a clean life and a clean body. Out of a defiled mind proceeds a defiled life and a corrupt body. Thought is the fount[1] of action, life, and manifestation; make the fountain pure, and all will be pure.

Change of diet will not help a man who will not change his thoughts. When a man makes his thoughts pure, he no longer desires impure food.

Clean thoughts make clean habits. The so-called saint who does not wash his body is not a saint. He who has strengthened and purified his thoughts does not need to consider the malevolent microbe.

If you would protect your body, guard your mind. If you would renew your body, beautify your mind. Thoughts of malice, envy, disappointment, despondency, rob the body of its health and grace. A sour face does not come by chance; it is made by sour thoughts. Wrinkles that mar[2] are drawn by folly, passion, and pride.

I know a woman of ninety-six who has the bright, innocent face of a girl. I know a man well under middle age whose face is drawn into inharmonious contours. The one is the result of a sweet and sunny disposition; the other is the outcome of passion and discontent.

As you cannot have a sweet and wholesome abode unless you admit the air and sunshine freely into your rooms, so a strong body and a bright, happy, or serene countenance can only result from the free admittance into the mind of thoughts of joy and goodwill and serenity.

---

[1] The source of.
[2] Ruin or disfigure.

Effect of Thought on Health . . .

On the faces of the aged there are wrinkles made by sympathy; others by strong and pure thought, and others are carved by passion: who cannot distinguish them? With those who have lived righteously, age is calm, peaceful, and softly mellowed, like the setting sun. I have recently seen a philosopher on his deathbed. He was not old except in years. He died as sweetly and peacefully as he had lived.

There is no physician like cheerful thought for dissipating the ills of the body; there is no comforter to compare with goodwill for dispersing the shadows of grief and sorrow. To live continually in thoughts of ill-will, cynicism, suspicion, and envy, is to be confined in a self-made prison-hole. But to think well of all, to be cheerful with all, to patiently learn to find the good in all—such unselfish thoughts are the very portals of heaven; and to dwell day by day in thoughts of peace toward every creature will bring abounding peace to their possessor.

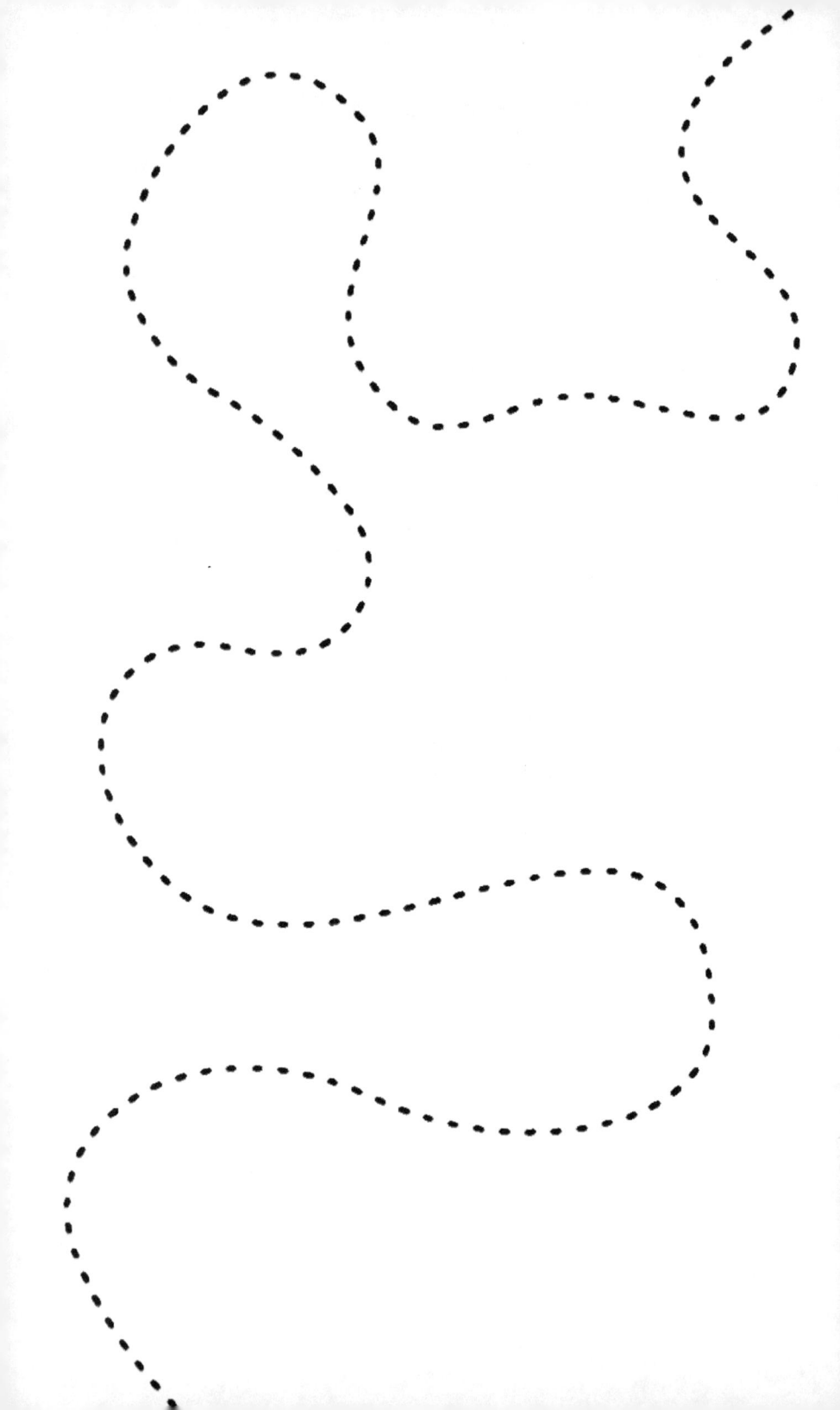

Thought & Purpose

Until thought is linked with purpose there is no intelligent accomplishment. With the majority the barque[1] of thought is allowed to "drift" upon the ocean of life. Aimlessness is a vice, and such drifting must not continue for him who would steer clear of catastrophe and destruction.

They who have no central purpose in their life fall an easy prey to petty worries, fears, troubles, and self-pityings, all of which are indications of weakness, which lead, just as surely as deliberately planned sins (though by a different route), to failure, unhappiness, and loss, for weakness cannot persist in a power-evolving universe.

A man should conceive of a legitimate purpose in his heart, and set out to accomplish it. He should make this purpose the centralizing point of his thoughts. It may take the form of a spiritual ideal, or it may be a worldly object, according to his nature at the time being; but whichever it is, he should steadily focus his thought-forces upon the object, which he has set before him. He should make this purpose his supreme duty, and should devote himself to

---

[1] In this context, a sailing ship or boat.

its attainment, not allowing his thoughts to wander away into ephemeral fancies, longings, and imaginings. This is the royal road to self-control and true concentration of thought. Even if he fails again and again to accomplish his purpose (as he necessarily must until weakness is overcome), the *strength of character gained* will be the measure of his *true* success, and this will form a new starting-point for future power and triumph.

Those who are not prepared for the apprehension of a *great* purpose should fix the thoughts upon the faultless performance of their duty, no matter how insignificant their task may appear. Only in this way can the thoughts be gathered and focused, and resolution and energy be developed, which being done, there is nothing which may not be accomplished.

The weakest soul, knowing its own weakness, and believing this truth—*that strength can only be developed by effort and practice*, will, thus believing, at once begin to exert itself, and, adding effort to effort, patience to patience, and strength to strength, will never cease to develop, and will at last grow divinely strong.

As the physically weak man can make himself strong by careful and patient training, so the man of weak thoughts can make them strong by exercising himself in right thinking.

To put away aimlessness and weakness, and to begin to think with purpose, is to enter the ranks of those strong ones who only recognize failure as one of the pathways to attainment; who make all conditions serve them, and who think strongly, attempt fearlessly, and accomplish masterfully.

Having conceived of his purpose, a man should

Thought & Purpose

mentally mark out a *straight* pathway to its achievement, looking neither to the right nor the left. Doubts and fears should be rigorously excluded; they are disintegrating elements which break up the straight line of effort, rendering it crooked, ineffectual, useless. Thoughts of doubt and fear never accomplished anything, and never can. They always lead to failure. Purpose, energy, power to do, and all strong thoughts cease when doubt and fear creep in.

The will to do springs from the knowledge that we *can* do. Doubt and fear are the great enemies of knowledge, and he who encourages them, who does not slay them, thwarts himself at every step.

He who has conquered doubt and fear has conquered failure. His every thought is allied with power, and all difficulties are bravely met and wisely overcome. His purposes are seasonably planted, and they bloom and bring forth fruit, which does not fall prematurely to the ground.

Thought allied fearlessly to purpose becomes creative force: he who *knows* this is ready to become something higher and stronger than a mere bundle of wavering thoughts and fluctuating sensations; he who *does* this has become the conscious and intelligent wielder of his mental powers.

The Thought-Factor in Achievement

All that a man achieves and all that he fails to achieve is the direct result of his own thoughts. In a justly ordered universe, where loss of equipoise[1] would mean total destruction, individual responsibility must be absolute. A man's weakness and strength, purity and impurity, are his own, and not another man's; they are brought about by himself, and not by another; and they can only be altered by himself, never by another. His condition is also his own, and not another man's. His suffering and his happiness are evolved from within. As he thinks, so he is; as he continues to think, so he remains.

A strong man cannot help a weaker unless that weaker is *willing* to be helped, and even then the weak man must become strong of himself; he must, by his own efforts, develop the strength which he admires in another. None but himself can alter his condition.

It has been usual for men to think and to say, "Many men are slaves because one is an oppressor; let us hate the oppressor." Now, however, there is amongst

---
[1] Balance.

an increasing few a tendency to reverse this judgment, and to say, "One man is an oppressor because many are slaves; let us despise the slaves."

The truth is that oppressor and slave are cooperators in ignorance, and, while seeming to afflict each other, are in reality afflicting themselves. A perfect Knowledge perceives the action of law in the weakness of the oppressed and the misapplied power of the oppressor; a perfect Love, seeing the suffering, which both states entail, condemns neither; a perfect Compassion embraces both oppressor and oppressed.

He who has conquered weakness, and has put away all selfish thoughts, belongs neither to oppressor nor oppressed. He is free.

A man can only rise, conquer, and achieve by lifting up his thoughts. He can only remain weak, abject,[2] and miserable by refusing to lift up his thoughts.

Before a man can achieve anything, even in worldly things, he must lift his thoughts above slavish animal indulgence. He may not, in order to succeed, give up *all* animality and selfishness, by any means; but a portion of it must, at least, be sacrificed. A man whose first thought is bestial indulgence could neither think clearly nor plan methodically; he could not find and develop his latent resources, and would fail in any undertaking. Not having commenced manfully to control his thoughts, he is not in a position to control affairs and to adopt serious responsibilities. He is not fit to act independently and stand alone. But he is limited only by the thoughts which he chooses.

There can be no progress, no achievement without sacrifice, and a man's worldly success will be in the

---

[2] Despicable; without pride or dignity.

The Thought-Factor in Achievement

measure that he sacrifices his confused animal thoughts, and fixes his mind on the development of his plans, and the strengthening of his resolution and self-reliance. And the higher he lifts his thoughts, the more manly, upright, and righteous he becomes, the greater will be his success, the more blessed and enduring will be his achievements.

The universe does not favor the greedy, the dishonest, the vicious, although on the mere surface it may sometimes appear to do so; it helps the honest, the magnanimous,[3] the virtuous. All the great Teachers of the ages have declared this in varying forms, and to prove and know it a man has but to persist in making himself more and more virtuous by lifting up his thoughts.

Intellectual achievements are the result of thought consecrated to the search for knowledge, or for the beautiful and true in life and nature. Such achievements may be sometimes connected with vanity and ambition, but they are not the outcome of those characteristics; they are the natural outgrowth of long and arduous effort, and of pure and unselfish thoughts.

Spiritual achievements are the consummation of holy aspirations. He who lives constantly in the conception of noble and lofty thoughts, who dwells upon all that is pure and unselfish, will, as surely as the sun reaches its zenith and the moon its full, become wise and noble in character, and rise into a position of influence and blessedness.

Achievement, of whatever kind, is the crown of effort, the diadem[4] of thought. By the aid of self-control, resolution, purity, righteousness, and well-directed thought a

---

[3] Forgiving and generous.
[4] An ornamental headband worn as a symbol of royalty.

man ascends; by the aid of animality, indolence, impurity, corruption, and confusion of thought a man descends.

A man may rise to high success in the world, and even to lofty altitudes in the spiritual realm, and again descend into weakness and wretchedness by allowing arrogant, selfish, and corrupt thoughts to take possession of him.

Victories attained by right thought can only be maintained by watchfulness. Many give way when success is assured, and rapidly fall back into failure.

All achievements, whether in the business, intellectual, or spiritual world, are the result of definitely directed thought, are governed by the same law and are of the same method; the only difference lies in *the object of attainment*.

He who would accomplish little must sacrifice little; he who would achieve much must sacrifice much; he who would attain highly must sacrifice greatly.

Visions & Ideals

The dreamers are the saviors of the world. As the visible world is sustained by the invisible, so men, through all their trials and sins and sordid vocations, are nourished by the beautiful visions of their solitary dreamers. Humanity cannot forget its dreamers; it cannot let their ideals fade and die; it lives in them; it knows them as the *realities* which it shall one day see and know.

Composer, sculptor, painter, poet, prophet, sage, these are the makers of the after-world, the architects of heaven. The world is beautiful because they have lived; without them, laboring humanity would perish.

He who cherishes a beautiful vision, a lofty ideal in his heart, will one day realize it. Columbus cherished a vision of another world, and he discovered it;[1] Copernicus fostered the vision of a multiplicity of worlds and a wider universe, and he revealed it;[2] Buddha beheld the

---

[1] Christopher Columbus (1451–1506) was an Italian explorer and navigator who completed four voyages across the Atlantic Ocean leading to the first known European contact with the Caribbean, Central America, and South America.

[2] Nicolaus Copernicus (1473–1543) was a Renaissance polymath who formulated a model of the universe that placed the Sun rather than Earth at its center.

vision of a spiritual world of stainless beauty and perfect peace, and he entered into it.

Cherish your visions; cherish your ideals; cherish the music that stirs in your heart, the beauty that forms in your mind, the loveliness that drapes your purest thoughts, for out of them will grow all delightful conditions, all heavenly environment; of these, if you but remain true to them, your world will at last be built.

To desire is to obtain; to aspire is to achieve. Shall man's basest desires receive the fullest measure of gratification, and his purest aspirations starve for lack of sustenance? Such is not the Law: such a condition of things can never obtain: "Ask and receive."

Dream lofty dreams, and as you dream, so shall you become. Your Vision is the promise of what you shall one day be; your Ideal is the prophecy of what you shall at last unveil.

The greatest achievement was at first and for a time a dream. The oak sleeps in the acorn; the bird waits in the egg; and in the highest vision of the soul a waking angel stirs. Dreams are the seedlings of realities.

Your circumstances may be uncongenial,[3] but they shall not long remain so if you but perceive an Ideal and strive to reach it. You cannot travel *within* and stand still *without*. Here is a youth hard pressed by poverty and labor; confined long hours in an unhealthy workshop; unschooled, and lacking all the arts of refinement. But he dreams of better things; he thinks of intelligence, of refinement, of grace and beauty. He conceives of, mentally builds up, an ideal condition of life; the vision of a wider liberty and a larger scope takes possession of him;

---

[3] Unsuitable; unfavorable.

Visions & Ideals

unrest urges him to action, and he utilizes all his spare time and means, small though they are, to the development of his latent powers and resources. Very soon so altered has his mind become that the workshop can no longer hold him. It has become so out of harmony with his mentality that it falls out of his life as a garment is cast aside, and, with the growth of opportunities which fit the scope of his expanding powers, he passes out of it forever. Years later we see this youth as a full-grown man. We find him a master of certain forces of the mind which he wields with worldwide influence and almost unequaled power. In his hands he holds the cords of gigantic responsibilities; he speaks, and lo! lives are changed; men and women hang upon his words and remold their characters, and, sunlike, he becomes the fixed and luminous center round which innumerable destinies revolve. He has realized the Vision of his youth. He has become one with his Ideal.

And you, too, youthful reader, will realize the Vision (not the idle wish) of your heart, be it base or beautiful, or a mixture of both, for you will always gravitate toward that which you, secretly, most love. Into your hands will be placed the exact results of your own thoughts; you will receive that which you earn; no more, no less. Whatever your present environment may be, you will fall, remain, or rise with your thoughts, your Vision, your Ideal. You will become as small as your controlling desire; as great as your dominant aspiration: in the beautiful words of Stanton Kirkham Davis:[4]

---

[4] Stanton Davis Kirkham (1868–1944) was a French-American naturalist, philosopher, ornithologist (one who studies birds), and author.

"You may be keeping accounts, and presently you shall walk out of the door that for so long has seemed to you the barrier of your ideals, and shall find yourself before an audience—the pen still behind your ear, the ink-stains on your fingers—and then and there shall pour out the torrent of your inspiration. You may be driving sheep, and you shall wander to the city—bucolic and open-mouthed; shall wander under the intrepid guidance of the spirit into the studio of the master, and after a time he shall say, 'I have nothing more to teach you.' And now you have become the master, who did so recently dream of great things while driving sheep. You shall lay down the saw and the plane to take upon yourself the regeneration of the world."[5]

The thoughtless, the ignorant, and the indolent, seeing only the apparent effects of things and not the things themselves, talk of luck, of fortune, and chance. Seeing a man grow rich, they say, "How lucky he is!" Observing another become intellectual, they exclaim, "How highly favored he is!" And noting the saintly character and wide influence of another, they remark, "How chance aids him at every turn!" They do not see the trials and failures and struggles which these men have voluntarily encountered in order to gain their experience; have no knowledge of the sacrifices they have made, of the undaunted efforts they have put forth, of the faith they have exercised, that they might overcome the apparently insurmountable, and realize the Vision of their heart. They do not know

---

[5] Borrowed from Chapter 12 of Kirkham's *Where Dwells the Soul Serene* (1900).

Visions & Ideals

the darkness and the heartaches; they only see the light and joy, and call it "luck"; do not see the long and arduous journey, but only behold the pleasant goal, and call it "good fortune"; do not understand the process, but only perceive the result, and call it "chance."

In all human affairs there are *efforts*, and there are *results*, and the strength of the effort is the measure of the result. Chance is not. "Gifts," powers, material, intellectual, and spiritual possessions are the fruits of effort; they are thoughts completed, objects accomplished, visions realized.

The Vision that you glorify in your mind, the Ideal that you enthrone in your heart—this you will build your life by, this you will become.

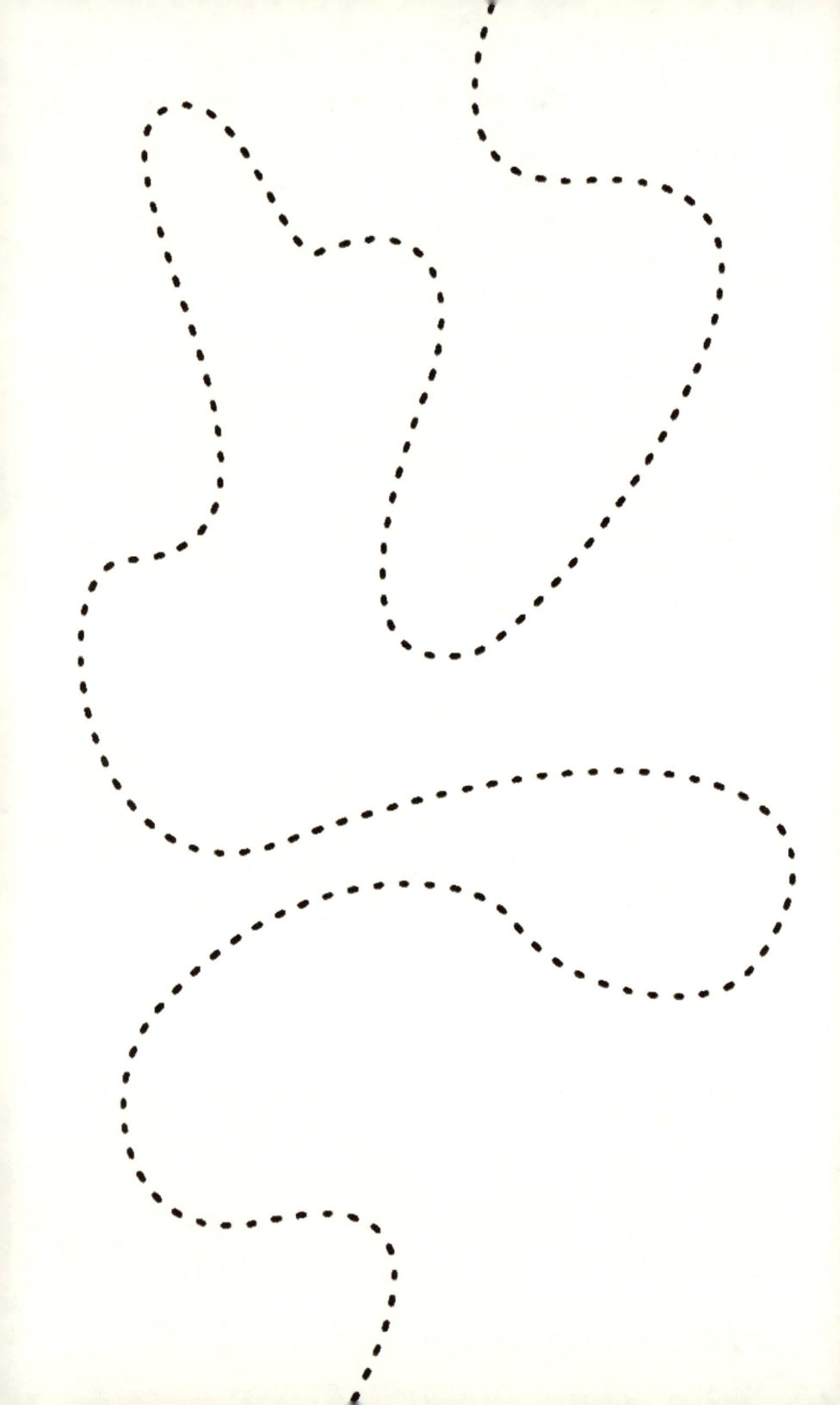

Serenity

Calmness of mind is one of the beautiful jewels of wisdom. It is the result of long and patient effort in self-control. Its presence is an indication of ripened experience, and of a more than ordinary knowledge of the laws and operations of thought.

A man becomes calm in the measure that he understands himself as a thought-evolved being, for such knowledge necessitates the understanding of others as the result of thought, and as he develops a right understanding, and sees more and more clearly the internal relations of things by the action of cause and effect, he ceases to fuss and fume and worry and grieve, and remains poised, steadfast, serene.

The calm man, having learned how to govern himself, knows how to adapt himself to others; and they, in turn, reverence[1] his spiritual strength, and feel that they can learn of him and rely upon him. The more tranquil a man becomes, the greater is his success, his influence, his power for good. Even the ordinary trader will find his business prosperity increase as he develops a greater

---

[1] Revere; regard with deep or profound respect and admiration.

self-control and equanimity,[2] for people will always prefer to deal with a man whose demeanor is strongly equable.[3]

The strong, calm man is always loved and revered. He is like a shade-giving tree in a thirsty land, or a sheltering rock in a storm. "Who does not love a tranquil heart, a sweet-tempered, balanced life? It does not matter whether it rains or shines, or what changes come to those possessing these blessings, for they are always sweet, serene, and calm. That exquisite poise of character, which we call serenity is the last lesson of culture, the fruitage of the soul. It is precious as wisdom, more to be desired than gold—yea, than even fine gold. How insignificant mere money-seeking looks in comparison with a serene life—a life that dwells in the ocean of Truth, beneath the waves, beyond the reach of tempests, in the Eternal Calm!

"How many people we know who sour their lives, who ruin all that is sweet and beautiful by explosive tempers, who destroy their poise of character, and make bad blood! It is a question whether the great majority of people do not ruin their lives and mar their happiness by lack of self-control. How few people we meet in life who are well-balanced, who have that exquisite poise which is characteristic of the finished character!"

Yes, humanity surges with uncontrolled passion, is tumultuous with ungoverned grief, is blown about by anxiety and doubt only the wise man, only he whose thoughts are controlled and purified, makes the winds and the storms of the soul obey him.

---

[2] Calmness of mind.
[3] Even-tempered and unvarying.

Serenity

Tempest-tossed souls, wherever ye may be, under whatsoever conditions ye may live, know this—in the ocean of life the isles of Blessedness are smiling, and the sunny shore of your ideal awaits your coming. Keep your hand firmly upon the helm of thought. In the barque of your soul reclines the commanding Master; He does but sleep; wake Him. Self-control is strength; Right Thought is mastery; Calmness is power. Say unto your heart, "Peace, be still!"

Out from the Heart

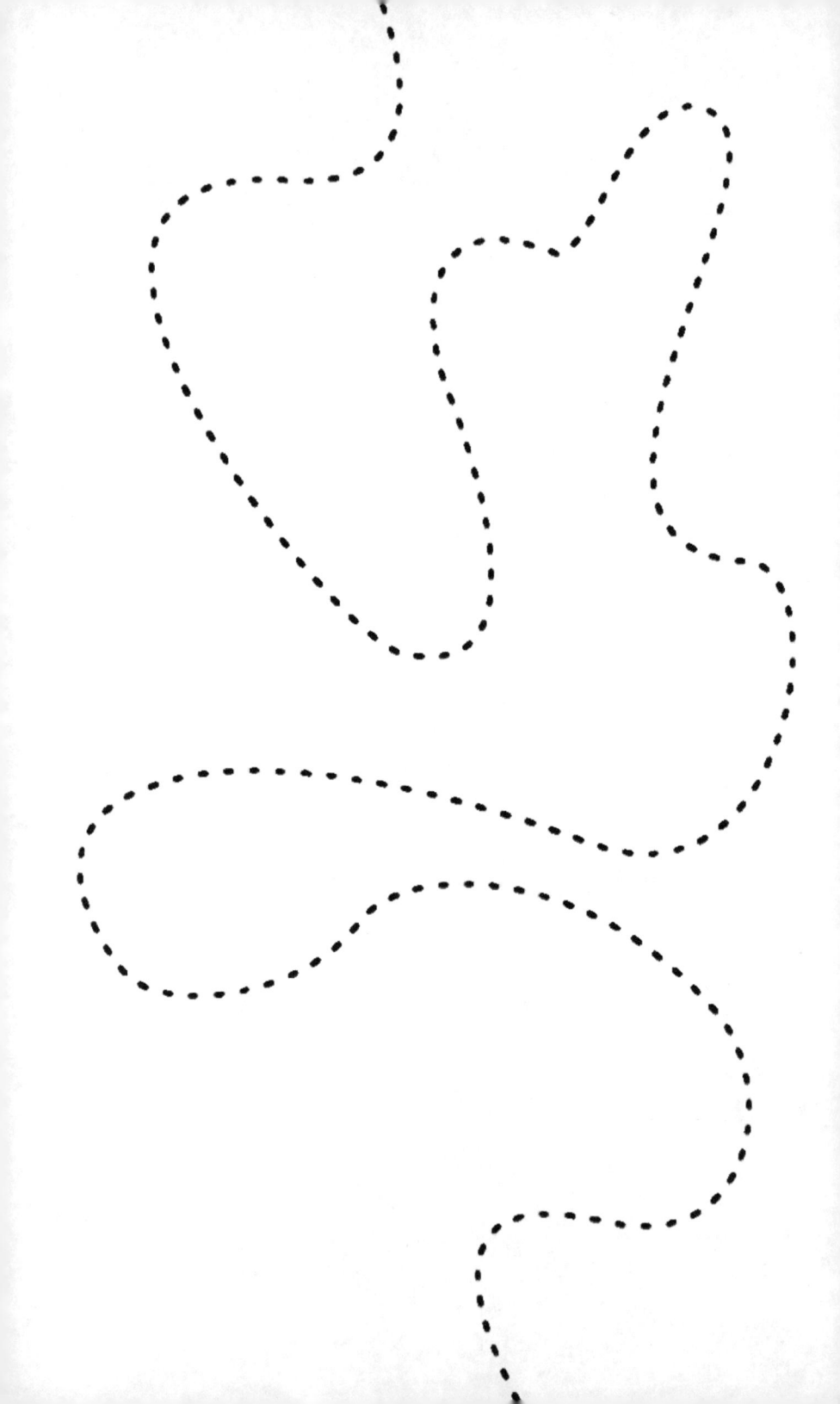

Foreword

Confucius[1] said, "The perfecting of one's self is the fundamental base of all progress and all moral development," a maxim as profound and comprehensive as it is simple, practical, and uninvolved, for there is no surer way to knowledge, nor no better way to help the world than by perfecting one's self. Nor is there any nobler work or higher science than that of self-perfection. He who studies how to become faultless, who strives to be pure-hearted, who aims at the possession of a calm, wise, and seeing mind, engages in the most sublime task that man can undertake, and the results of which are perceptible in a well-ordered, blessed, and beautiful life.

James Allen
Broad Park Avenue,
Ilfracombe,
England

---

[1] Confucius (c.551–c.479 BC) was a Chinese philosopher traditionally considered the paragon of Chinese sages, and much of the shared East Asian cultural heritage originates in his philosophy and teachings.

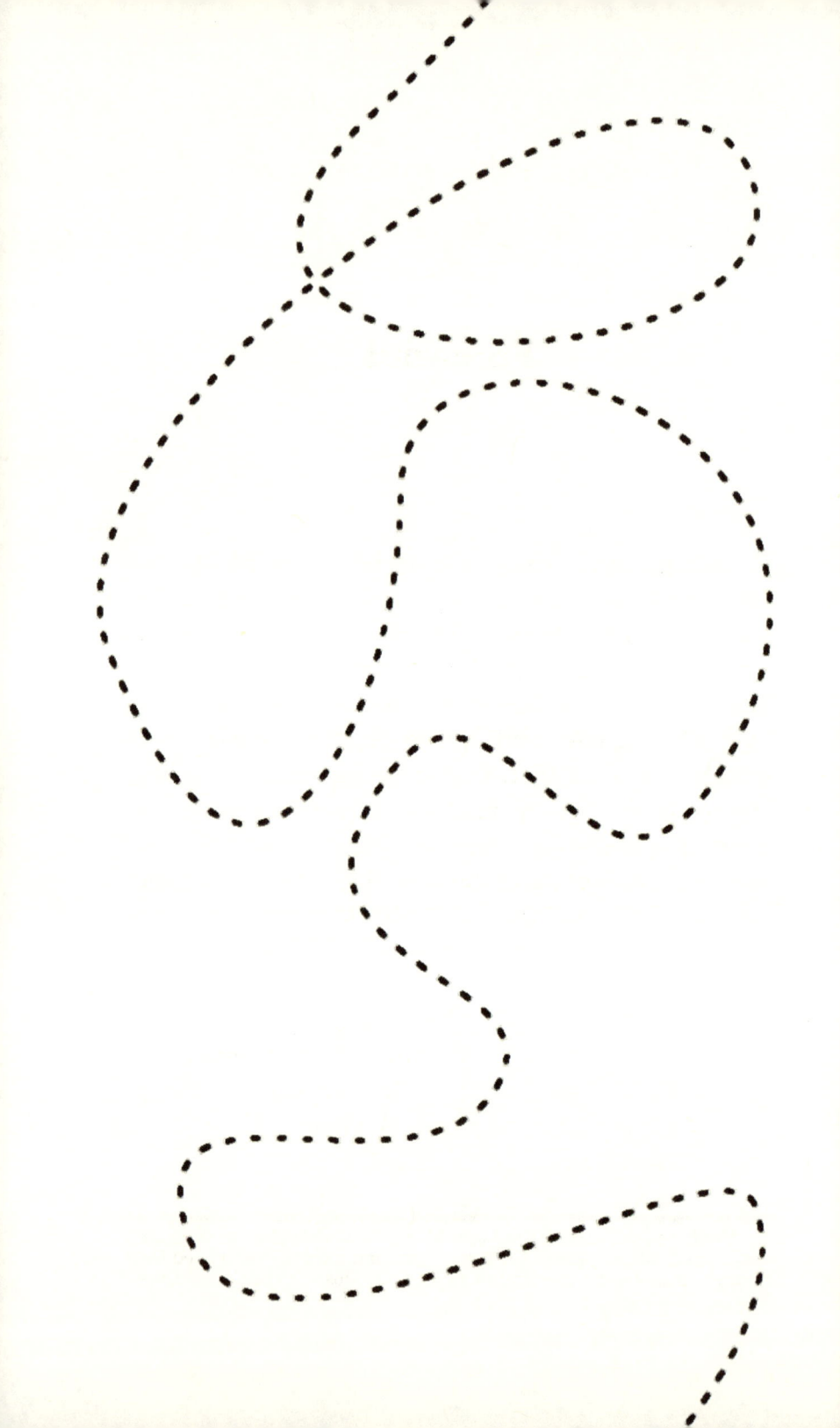

The Heart & The Life

As the heart, so is the life. The within is ceaselessly becoming the without. Nothing remains unrevealed. That which is hidden is but for a time; it ripens and comes forth at last. Seed, tree, blossom, and fruit is the fourfold[1] order of the universe. From the state of a man's heart proceed the conditions of his life; his thoughts blossom into deeds, and his deeds bear the fruitage of character and destiny.

Life is ever unfolding from within, and revealing itself to the light, and thoughts engendered in the heart at last reveal themselves in words, actions, and things accomplished.

As the fountain from the hidden spring, so issues man's life from the secret recesses of his heart. All that he is and does is generated there. All that he will be and do will take its rise there.

Sorrow and gladness, suffering and enjoyment, hope and fear, hatred and love, ignorance and enlightenment, are nowhere but in the heart; they are solely mental conditions.

---
[1] Four-part or four parts.

Out from the Heart

Man is the keeper of his heart; the watcher of his mind; the solitary sentinel of his citadel of life. As such, he can be diligent or negligent. He can keep his heart more and more carefully; he can more strenuously watch and purify his mind; and he can guard himself against the thinking of unrighteous thoughts: this is the way of enlightenment and bliss. On the other hand, he can live loosely and carelessly, neglecting the supreme task of rightly ordering his life: this is the way of self-delusion and suffering.

Let a man realize that life in its totality proceeds from the mind, and lo, the way of blessedness is opened up to him! For he will then discover that he possesses the power to rule his mind, and to fashion it in accordance with his Ideal. So will he elect to strongly and steadfastly walk those pathways of thought and action which are altogether excellent; to him life will become beautiful and sacred; and, sooner or later, he will put to flight all evil, confusion, and suffering; for it is impossible for a man to fall short of liberation, enlightenment, and peace, who guards with unwearying diligence the gateway of his heart.

The Nature and Power of Mind

Mind is the arbiter[1] of life; it is the creator and shaper of conditions, and the recipient of its own results. It contains within itself both the power to create illusion and to perceive reality.

Mind is the infallible weaver of destiny; thought is the thread, good and evil deeds are the warp and woof,[2] and the web, woven upon the loom of life, is character. Mind clothes itself in garments of its own making.

Man, as a mental being, possesses all the powers of mind, and is furnished with illimitable[3] choice. He learns by experience, and he can accelerate or retard his experience. He is not arbitrarily bound at any point, but he has bound himself at many points, and having bound himself he can, when he chooses, liberate himself. He can become bestial or pure, ignoble or noble, foolish or wise, just as he chooses. He can, by recurring practice,

---

[1] Judge or umpire.
[2] A phrase meaning the underlying structure or foundation of something, taken from the weaving of fabric where the warp are threads that run lengthwise, and the woof (or weft) are threads that run crosswise.
[3] Without limits.

form habits, and he can, by renewed effort, break them off. He can surround himself with illusions until Truth is completely lost, and he can destroy those illusions one after another until Truth is entirely recovered. His possibilities are limitless; his freedom is complete.

It is in the nature of mind to create its own conditions, and to choose the states in which it shall dwell. It also has the power to alter any condition and to abandon any state, and this it is continually doing as it gathers knowledge of state after state by repeated choice and exhaustive experience.

Inward processes of thought makeup the sum of character and life, and man can modify and alter these processes by bringing will and effort to bear upon them. The bonds of habit, impotence, and sin are self-made, and can only be destroyed by one's self; they exist nowhere but in one's mind, and although they are directly related to outward things, they have no real existence in those things. The outer is molded and vivified[4] by the inner, and never the inner by the outer. Temptation does not arise in the outer object, but *in the lust of the mind for that object*; nor do suffering and sorrow inhere[5] in the external things and happenings of life, but in an undisciplined attitude of mind toward those things and happenings. The mind that is disciplined by Purity and fortified by Wisdom, avoids all those lusts and desires which are inseparably bound up with affliction, and so arrives at enlightenment and peace.

To condemn others as evil, and to rail against outside conditions as the source of evil, increases, and does not

---

[4] Brought to life; animated.
[5] Exist permanently.

The Nature and Power of Mind

lessen, the world's suffering and unrest. The outer is but the shadow and effect of the inner, and when the heart is pure all outward things are pure.

All growth and life is from within outward; all decay and death is from without inward; this is a universal law. All evolution proceeds from within. All adjustment must take place within. He who ceases to strive against others, and employs his powers in the transformation, regeneration, and development of his own mind, conserves his energies and preserves himself; and as he succeeds in harmonizing his own mind, he leads others by consideration and charity into a like blessed state, for not by assuming authority and guidance over other minds is the way of enlightenment and peace discovered, but by exercising a lawful authority over one's own, and by guiding one's self in pathways of steadfast and lofty virtue.

A man's life proceeds from his heart, his mind: he has compounded that mind by his own thoughts and deeds: it is in his power to re-fashion that mind by his choice of thought: he can therefore transform his life. Let us see how this is to be done.

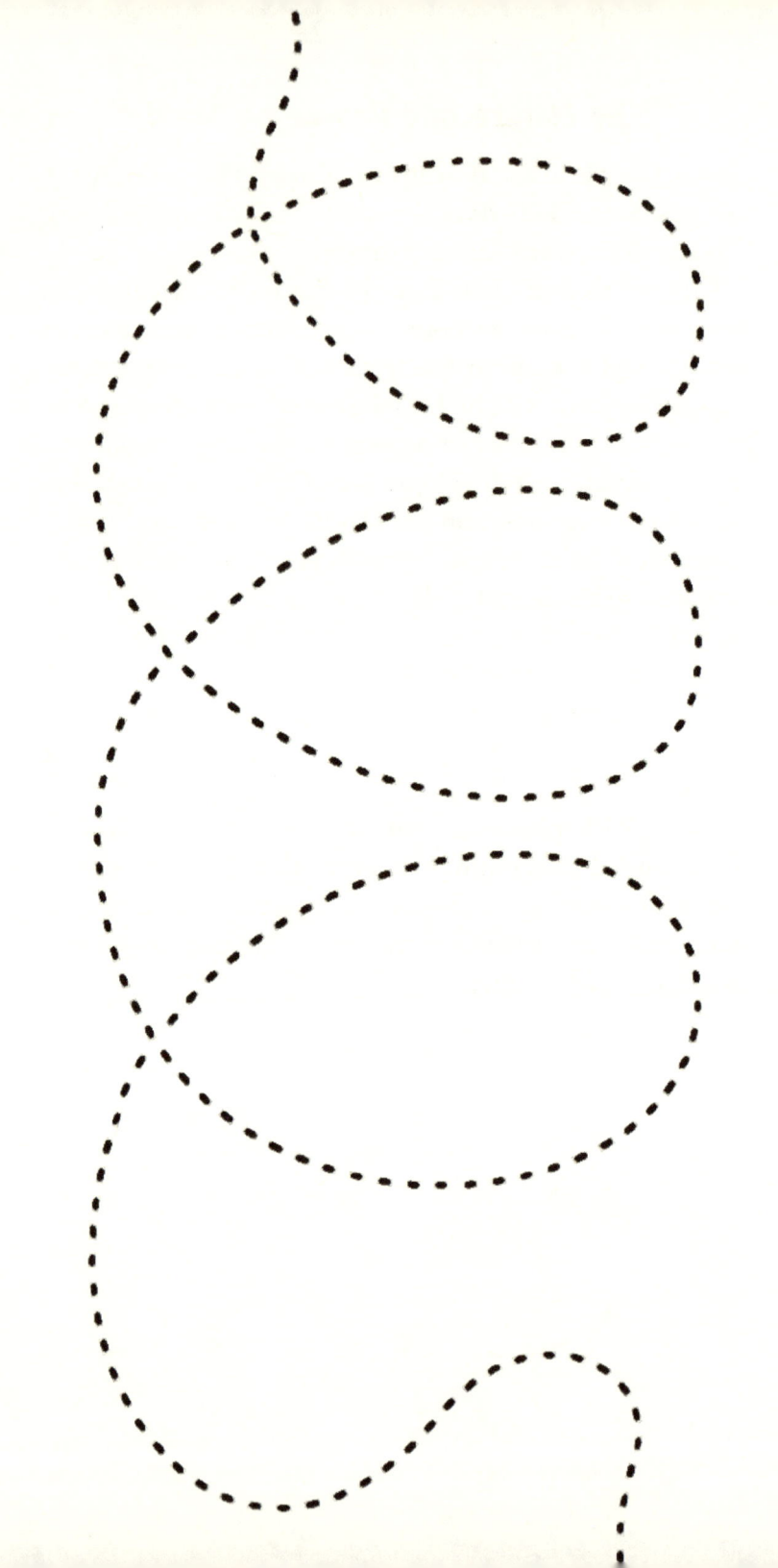

Formation of Habit

Every established mental condition is an *acquired habit*, and it has become such by continuous repetition of thought. Despondency and cheerfulness, anger and calmness, covetousness[1] and generosity — indeed, all states of mind — are habits built up by choice, until they have become automatic. A thought constantly repeated at last becomes a fixed habit of the mind, and from such habits proceeds the life.

It is in the nature of the mind to acquire knowledge by the repetition of its experiences. A thought which it is very difficult, at first, to hold and to dwell upon, at last becomes, by constantly being held in the mind, a natural and habitual condition. Just as a boy, when commencing to learn a trade, cannot even handle his tools aright, much less use them correctly, but after long repetition and practice plies them with perfect ease and consummate skill, so a state of mind, at first apparently impossible of realization, is, by perseverance and practice, at last acquired and built into the character as a natural and spontaneous condition.

---

[1] An eager and overwhelming desire to possess that which belongs to someone else.

In this power of the mind to form and re-form its habits, its conditions, is contained the basis of man's salvation, and the open door to perfect liberty by the mastery of self, for as a man has the power to form harmful habits, so he has the same power to create habits that are essentially good. And here we come to a point which needs some elucidating,[2] and which calls for deep and earnest thought on the part of my reader.

It is commonly said to be easier to do wrong than right, to sin than to be holy; such condition has come to be regarded, almost universally, as axiomatic,[3] and no less a teacher than the Buddha has said: — "Bad deeds, and deeds hurtful to ourselves, are easy to do; what is beneficial and good, that is very difficult to do," — and as regards humanity generally, this is true, but it is only true as a passing experience, a fleeting factor in human evolution; it is not a fixed condition of things, is not of the nature of an eternal truth. It is easier for men to do wrong than right, because of the prevalence of *ignorance*, because the true nature of things, and the essence and meaning of life, are not apprehended. When a child is learning to write, it is extremely easy for it to hold the pen wrongly, and to form its letters incorrectly, but it is painfully difficult to hold the pen and to write properly; and this because of the child's ignorance of the art of writing, which can only be dispelled by persistent effort and practice, until, at last, it becomes natural and easy to hold the pen properly, and to write correctly, and difficult, as well as altogether unnecessary, to do the wrong thing. It is the same in the vital things of mind and life. To think and do rightly requires much practice and renewed effort,

---

[2] Explaining, to make clear.
[3] Self-evident.

Formation of Habit

but the time at last comes when it becomes habitual and easy to think and do rightly, and difficult, as it is then seen to be altogether unnecessary, to do that which is wrong.

Just as an artisan becomes, by practice, accomplished in his craft, so a man can become, by practice, accomplished in goodness; it is entirely a matter of forming new habits of thought, and he to whom right thoughts have become easy and natural, and wrong thoughts and acts difficult to do, has attained to the highest virtue, to pure, spiritual knowledge.

It is easy and natural for men to sin, because they have formed, by incessant repetition, harmful and unenlightened habits of thought. It is very difficult for the thief to refrain from stealing when opportunity occurs, because he has lived so long in covetous and avaricious[4] thoughts; but such difficulty does not exist for the honest man who has lived so long in upright and honest thoughts, and has thereby become enlightened as to the wrong, folly, and fruitlessness of theft, that even the remotest idea of stealing does not enter his mind. The sin of theft is a very extreme one, and I have introduced it in order to more clearly illustrate the force and formation of habit; but all sins and virtues are formed in the same way. Anger and impatience are natural and easy to thousands of people because they are constantly repeating the angry and impatient thought and act, and with each repetition the habit is more firmly established and more deeply rooted. Calmness and patience can become habitual in the same way — by first grasping, through effort, a calm and patient thought, and then continuously thinking it, and living in it, until "use becomes second nature," and

---

[4] Extreme desire for wealth or material possessions; covetousness (see first footnote on previous page).

ch. ends next p.

anger and impatience pass away forever. It is thus that every wrong thought may be expelled from the mind; thus that every untrue act may be destroyed; thus that every sin may be overcome.

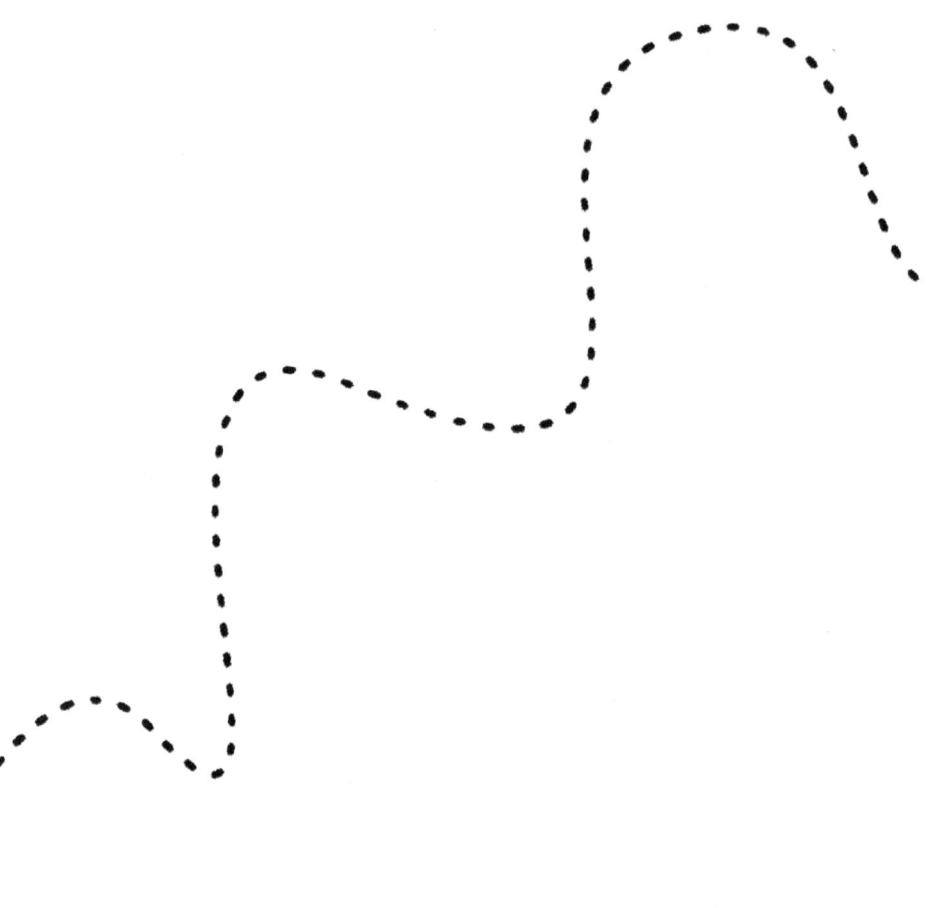

Doing & Knowing

Let a man realize that his life, in its totality, proceeds from his mind, and that that mind is a combination of habits which he can, by patient effort, modify to any extent, and over which he can thus gain complete ascendancy and control, and he has at once obtained possession of the key which shall open the door to his complete emancipation.[1]

But emancipation from the ills of life (which are the ills of one's mind) is a matter of steady growth from within, and not a sudden acquisition from without. Hourly and daily must the mind be trained to think stainless thoughts, and to adopt right and dispassionate attitudes under those circumstances in which it is prone to fall into wrong and passion. Like the patient sculptor upon his marble, the aspirant[2] to the Right Life must gradually work upon the crude material of his mind until he has wrought out of it the Ideal of his holiest dreams.

In working toward such supreme accomplishment, it is necessary to commence at the lowest and easiest steps,

[1] Liberation; the act of being freed.
[2] An ambitious person who eagerly seeks to achieve something.

and proceed by natural and progressive stages to the higher and more difficult. This law of growth, progress, evolution, unfoldment, by gradual and ever ascending stages, is absolute in every department of life, and in every human accomplishment, and where it is ignored, total failure will result. In acquiring learning, in learning a trade, or in pursuing a business, this law is fully recognized and minutely obeyed by all; but in acquiring Virtue, in learning Truth, and in pursuing the right conduct and knowledge of life, it is unrecognized and disobeyed by nearly all; hence, Virtue, Truth, and the Perfect Life remain unpracticed, unacquired, and unknown.

It is a common error to suppose that the Higher Life is a matter of reading, and the adoption of theological or metaphysical hypotheses, and that Spiritual Principles can be apprehended by this method. The Higher Life is a *higher living* in thought, word, and deed, and the knowledge of those Spiritual Principles, which are immanent[3] in man and in the universe can only be acquired after long discipline in the pursuit and practice of Virtue.

The lesser must be thoroughly grasped and understood before the greater can be known, and practice always precedes *real* knowledge. The schoolmaster never attempts to teach his pupils the abstract principles of mathematics at the commencement; he knows that by such a method teaching would be vain, and learning impossible. He first places before them a simple sum, and, having explained it, leaves them to *do it*. When, after repeated failures and ever-renewed effort, they have succeeded in doing it correctly, a more difficult task is set them, and then another and another; and not until the

---
[3] Inherent; existing within.

Doing & Knowing

pupils have, through many years of diligent application, mastered all the lessons in arithmetic, does he attempt to unfold to them the underlying mathematical principles.

In learning a trade, say that of a mechanic, the boy is not at first taught the principles of mechanics, but a simple tool is put into his hand and he is told how rightly to use it, and is then left to do it by effort and practice. As he succeeds in plying his tools correctly, more and more difficult tasks are set him, until, after several years of successful practice, he is prepared to study and grasp the principles of mechanics.

In a properly governed household, the child is first taught to be obedient, and to conduct itself properly under all circumstances. The child is not even told why it must do this, but is commanded to do it, and only after it has so far succeeded in doing what is right and proper, is it told *why* it should do it. No father would attempt to teach his child the principles of ethics before exacting from it the practice of filial[4] duty and social virtue.

Thus practice ever precedes knowledge even in the ordinary things of the world, and in spiritual things, in the living of the Higher Life, this law is rigid in its exactions. Virtue can only be known by *doing* and the knowledge of Truth can only be arrived at by perfecting oneself in the practice of Virtue, and to be complete in the practice and acquisition of Virtue is to be complete in the knowledge of Truth.

Truth can only be arrived at by daily and hourly doing the lessons of Virtue, beginning at the simplest, and passing on to the more difficult; and as a child patiently and obediently learns its lessons at school, constantly

---

[4] The relation of a child to a parent.

practicing, ever exerting itself until all failures and difficulties are surmounted, even so does the child of Truth apply himself to right-doing in thought and action, undaunted by failure, and made stronger by difficulties; and as he succeeds in acquiring Virtue, his mind unfolds itself in the knowledge of Truth, and it is a knowledge in which he can securely rest.

First Steps in the Higher Life

Seeing that the Path of Virtue is the Path of Knowledge, and that before the all-embracing Principles of Truth can be comprehended, perfection in the more lowly steps must be acquired, how, then, shall a disciple of Truth commence? How shall one who aspires to the righting of his mind and the purification of his heart — that heart which is the fountain and repository of all the issues of life — learn the lessons of Virtue, and thus build himself up in the strength of knowledge, destroying ignorance and the ills of life? What are the first lessons, the first steps? How are they learned? How are they practiced? How are they mastered and understood?

The first lessons consist in overcoming those wrong mental conditions which are most easily eradicated, and which are the common barriers to spiritual progress, as well as in practicing the simple domestic and social virtues; and the reader will be the better aided if I group and classify the first ten steps in three lessons as follows:

Out from the Heart

VICES TO BE OVERCOME AND ERADICATED

VICES OF THE BODY

1. Indolence. [Laziness.]   }   ***First Lesson***
2. Self-Indulgence.   Discipline of the Body

VICES OF THE TONGUE

1. Slander.
2. Gossip and idle conversation.   }   ***Second Lesson***
3. Abusive and unkind speech.   Discipline of
4. Levity, or irreverent speech.   Speech
5. Captiousness, or fault-finding speech.

VIRTUES TO BE PRACTICED AND ACQUIRED

1. Unselfish performance of duty.   }   ***Third Lesson***
2. Unswerving rectitude.   Discipline of
3. Unlimited forgiveness.   Inclination

    The two vices of the body, and five of the tongue, are so called because they are manifested in the body and tongue, and also because, by so definitely classifying them, the mind of the reader will be the better helped; but it must be clearly understood that these vices arise primarily in the mind, and are wrong conditions of heart worked out in the body and the tongue.

    The existence of such chaotic conditions is an indication that the mind is altogether unenlightened as to the

First Steps in the Higher Life

real meaning and purpose of life, and their eradication is the beginning of a virtuous, steadfast, and enlightened life.

But how shall they be overcome and eradicated? By first, and at once, checking and controlling their outward manifestations, by suppressing the wrong act; this will stimulate the mind to watchfulness and reflection until, by repeated practice, it will at last come to perceive and understand the dark and wrong conditions of mind, out of which such acts spring, and will abandon them entirely.

It will be seen that the first step in the discipline of the mind is the overcoming of indolence. This is the easiest step, and until it is perfectly accomplished, the other steps cannot be taken. The clinging to indolence constitutes a complete barrier to the Path of Truth. Indolence consists in giving the body more ease and sleep than it requires, in procrastinating, and in shirking and neglecting those things which should receive immediate attention. This condition of laziness must be overcome by rousing up the body at an early hour, giving it just the amount of sleep it requires for complete recuperation, and by doing, promptly and vigorously, every task and duty, no matter how small, as it comes along. On no account should food or drink be taken in bed, and to lie in bed after one has wakened, indulging in ease and reverie, is a habit fatal to promptness and resolution of character, and purity of mind. Nor should one attempt to do his thinking at such a time. Strong, pure, and true thinking is impossible under such circumstances. A man should go to bed to sleep, not to think. He should get up to think and work, not to sleep.

The next step is the overcoming of self-indulgence, or gluttony. The glutton is he who eats for animal gratification only, without considering the true end and object in eating, who eats more than his body requires, and is greedy after sweet things and rich dishes. Such undisciplined desire can only be overcome by reducing the quantity of food eaten, and the number of meals per day, and by resorting to a simple and uninvolved dietary.[1] Regular hours should be set apart for meals, and eating at other times should be rigidly avoided. Suppers should be abolished, as they are altogether unnecessary, and conduce to heavy sleep and cloudiness of mind. The pursuit of such a method of discipline will rapidly bring the hitherto ungoverned appetite under control, and as the sensual sin of self-indulgence is taken out of the mind, the right selection of food will be instinctively and infallibly adapted to the purified mental condition.

It should be well borne in mind that *change of heart* is the needful thing, and that any change of diet which does not subserve[2] this end is futile. Whilst one eats for enjoyment he is gluttonous. The heart must be purified of sensual craving and gustatory[3] lust.

When the body is well controlled and firmly guided; when that which is to be done is done vigorously; when no task or duty is delayed; when early rising has become a delight; when frugality, temperance, and abstinence are firmly established; when one is contented with the food which is put before him, no matter how scanty and plain, and the craving for gustatory pleasure is at an end — then are the first two steps in the Higher Life accomplished; then is the first great lesson in Truth

---

[1] Regulated diet.
[2] Promote; further.
[3] Pertaining to taste or sense of taste.

learned. Thus is established in the heart the foundation of a poised, self-governed, virtuous life.

The next lesson is the lesson of Virtuous Speech, in which are five orderly steps. The first step is the overcoming of slander. Slander consists in inventing or repeating evil reports about others, in exposing and magnifying the faults of others, or of absent friends, and in introducing unworthy insinuations. The elements of thoughtlessness, cruelty, insincerity, and untruthfulness enter into every slanderous act. He who aims at the living of the right life will commence to check the cruel word of slander before it has gone forth from his lips, and will then check and eliminate the insincere thought which gave rise to it. He will watch himself that he does not vilify any, and will refrain from disparaging and condemning the absent friend, whose face he has so recently kissed, or shaken his hand, or smiled into his face. He will not say *of* another that which he dare not say *to* him. Thus, coming at last to think sacredly of the character and reputation of others, he will destroy those wrong conditions of mind which give rise to slander.

The next step is the overcoming of gossip and idle conversation. Idle speech consists in talking about the private affairs of others, in talking merely to pass away the time, and in engaging in aimless and irrelevant conversation. Such an ungoverned condition of speech is the outcome of an ill-regulated mind. The man of virtue will bridle his tongue, and thus learn how rightly to govern the mind. He will not let his tongue run idly and foolishly, but will make his speech strong and pure, and will either talk with a purpose or remain silent.

Abusive and unkind speech is the next vice to be

ch. ends p. 69

overcome. The man who abuses and accuses others has himself wandered far from the Right Way. To hurl hard words and names at others is to sink deeply into folly. When a man is inclined to abuse and condemn others, let him restrain his tongue and look in upon himself. The virtuous man refrains from abuse and quarreling, and employs only words that are useful, necessary, pure, and true.

The next step is the overcoming of levity, or irreverent speech. Light and frivolous talking; the repeating of coarse jokes; the telling of vulgar stories, having no other purpose than to raise an empty laugh; offensive familiarity, and the employment of contemptuous and irreverent terms when speaking to or of others, and particularly of one's elders and those who rank as one's teachers, guardians, or superiors — all this will be put away by the lover of Virtue and Truth.

Upon the altar of irreverence absent friends and companions are immolated[4] for the passing excitement of a momentary laugh, and all the sanctity of life is sacrificed to the zest for ridicule. When respect toward others and the giving of reverence where reverence is due are abandoned, Virtue is abandoned. When modesty, gravity, and dignity are eliminated from speech and behavior, Truth is lost, yea, even its entrance-gate is hidden away and forgotten. Irreverence is degrading even in the young, but when it accompanies gray hairs, and appears in the demeanor of the preacher — this is indeed a piteous spectacle; and when this can be imitated and followed after, then are the blind leading the blind, then have elders and preacher and people lost their way.

---

[4] Sacrificed, especially by fire.

First Steps in the Higher Life

The virtuous man will be of grave and reverent speech; he will think and speak of the absent as he thinks and speaks of the dead — tenderly and sacredly; he will put away thoughtlessness, and watch that he does not sacrifice his dignity to gratify a passing impulse to lightness and frivolity. His mirth[5] will be pure and innocent, and his voice will become subdued and musical, and his soul be filled with grace and sweetness as he succeeds in conducting himself as becomes a man of Truth.

The last step in the second lesson is the overcoming of captiousness,[6] or fault-finding speech. This vice of the tongue consists in magnifying and harping on small or apparent faults, in foolish quibbling and hair-splitting, and in pursuing vain arguments based upon groundless suppositions, beliefs, and opinions. Life is short and real, and sin and sorrow and pain are not remedied by carping and contention. The man who is ever on the watch to catch at the words of others in order to contradict and controvert them, has yet to reach the higher way of holiness, the truer life of self-surrender. The man who is ever on the watch to check his own words in order to soften and purify them will find the higher way and the truer life; he will conserve his energies, maintain his composure of mind, and preserve within himself the spirit of Truth.

When the tongue is well controlled and wisely subdued; when selfish impulses and unworthy thoughts no longer rush to the tongue demanding utterance; when the speech has become harmless, pure, gentle, gracious, and purposeful, and no word is uttered but in sincerity

---

[5] Amusement and merriment, especially as expressed by laughter.
[6] To find and point out trivial faults or raise petty objections.

and truth — then are the five steps in virtuous speech accomplished, then is the second great lesson in Truth learned and mastered.

And now some will ask, "But why all this discipline of the body and restraint of the tongue? Surely the Higher Life can be realized and known without such strenuous labor, such incessant effort and watchfulness?" No, it cannot. In the spiritual as the material, nothing is done without labor, and the higher cannot be known until the lower is fulfilled. Can a man make a table before he has learned how to handle a tool and drive a nail? And can a man fashion his mind in accordance with Truth before he has overcome the slavery of his body? As the intricate subtleties of language cannot be apprehended and wielded before the alphabet and the simplest words are mastered, neither can the deep subtleties of the mind be understood and purified before the A B C of right conduct is perfectly acquired. As for the labor involved — does not the youth joyfully and patiently submit himself to a seven-years' apprenticeship in order to master a craft? And does he not day by day carefully and faithfully carry out every detail of his master's instructions, looking forward to the time when, perfected through obedience and practice, he shall be himself a master? Where is the man who sincerely aims at excellence in music, painting, literature, in any trade, business, or profession, who is not willing to give his whole life to the acquirement of his particular perfection? Shall, then, labor be considered where the very highest excellence is concerned — the excellence of Truth? He who says, "The Path which you point out is too difficult; I must have Truth without labor, salvation without effort," that man will not find his way

First Steps in the Higher Life

out of the confusions and sufferings of self-hood; he will not find the calm and well-fortified mind and the wisely ordered life. His love is for ease and enjoyment, and not for Truth. He who, deep in his heart, adores Truth, and aspires to know it, will consider no labor too great to be undertaken, but will adopt it joyfully and pursue it patiently, and by perseverance in practice he will come to the knowledge of Truth.

The necessity for this preliminary discipline of the body and tongue will be the more clearly perceived when it is fully understood that all these wrong outward conditions are merely the expressions of wrong conditions of heart. An indolent body means an indolent mind; an ill-regulated tongue reveals an ill-regulated mind, and the process of remedying the manifested condition is really a method of rectifying the inward state. Moreover, the overcoming of these conditions is only a small part of what is really involved in the process. The ceasing from evil leads to, and is inseparably connected with, the practice of good. While a man is overcoming indolence and self-indulgence, he is really cultivating and developing the virtues of abstinence, temperance, punctuality, and self-denial, and is acquiring that strength, energy, and resolution which are indispensable to the successful accomplishment of the higher tasks. While he is overcoming the vices of speech, he is developing the virtues of truthfulness, sincerity, reverence, kindliness, and self-control, and is gaining that mental steadiness and fixedness of purpose, without which the remoter subtleties of the mind cannot be regulated, and the higher stages of conduct and enlightenment cannot be reached. Also, as he learns to *do* right, his knowledge deepens, and his insight is intensified, and as the child's heart is glad when his school-task is mastered, so with each victory achieved, the man of virtue experiences a bliss which the seeker after pleasure and excitement can never know.

And now we come to the third lesson in the Higher Life, which consists in practicing and mastering, in one's daily life, three great fundamental Virtues, namely:

1. Unselfish Performance of Duty;
2. Unswerving Rectitude;[7] and
3. Unlimited Forgiveness.

Having prepared the mind by overcoming the more surface and chaotic conditions mentioned in the two first lessons, the striver after Virtue and Truth is now ready to enter upon greater and more difficult tasks, and to control and purify the deeper motives of the heart. Without the right performance of duty, the higher virtues cannot be known, and Truth cannot be apprehended. Duty is generally regarded as an irksome labor, a compulsory something which must be toiled through, or be in some way circumvented. This way of regarding Duty proceeds from a selfish condition of mind, and a wrong understanding of life. All duty should be regarded as sacred, and its faithful and unselfish performance one of the leading rules of conduct. All personal and selfish considerations should be extracted and cast away from the doing of one's duty, and when this is done, Duty ceases to be irksome, and becomes joyful. Duty is only irksome to him who craves some selfish enjoyment or benefit for himself. Let the man who is chafing under the irksomeness of his duty look to himself, and he will find that his wearisomeness proceeds, not from the duty itself, but from his selfish

---

[7] Righteousness; morally correct behavior or thinking.

desire to escape it. He who neglects duty, be it great or small, or of a public or private nature, neglects Virtue; he who in his heart rebels against Duty, rebels against Virtue. When Duty has become a thing of love, and when every particular duty is done accurately, faithfully, and dispassionately, there is much subtle selfishness removed from the heart, and a great step is taken toward the heights of Truth. The virtuous man concentrates his mind on the perfect doing of his own duty, and does not interfere with the duty of another.

The second step in the third lesson is the practice of Unswerving Rectitude. This Virtue must be firmly established in the mind, and so enter into every detail of a man's life. All dishonesty, deception, trickery, and misrepresentation must be forever put away, and the heart be purged of every vestige of insincerity and subterfuge. The least swerving from the path of rectitude is a deviation from Virtue. There must be no extravagance and exaggeration of speech, but the simple truth should be stated. Engaging in deception, no matter how apparently insignificant, for vain-glory, or with the hope of personal advantage, is a state of delusion which one should make efforts to dispel. It is demanded of the man of Virtue that he shall not only practice the most rigid honesty in thought, word, and deed, but that he shall be exact in his statements, omitting and adding nothing to the actual truth. In thus shaping his mind to the principle of Rectitude, he will gradually come to deal with people and things in a just and impartial spirit, considering equity before himself, and viewing all things with freedom from personal bias, passion, and prejudice. When the Virtue of Rectitude is fully practiced, acquired, and comprehended, so that all temptation to untruthfulness and insincerity has ceased, then is the heart made purer and nobler, then is character strengthened, and knowledge enlarged, and life takes on a new meaning and a new power. Thus is the second step accomplished.

The third step is the practice of Unlimited Forgiveness. This consists in overcoming the sense of injury which springs from vanity, selfishness, and pride; and in exercising disinterested charity and large-heartedness toward all. Spite, retaliation, and revenge are so utterly ignoble, and so small and foolish, as to be altogether unworthy of being noticed or harbored. No one who fosters such conditions in his heart can lift himself above folly and suffering, and guide his life aright. Only by casting them away, and ceasing to be moved by them, can a man's eyes be opened to the true way in life; only by developing a forgiving and charitable spirit can he hope to approach and perceive the strength and beauty of a well-ordered life. In the heart of the strongly virtuous man no feeling of personal injury can arise; he has put away all retaliation, and has no enemies; and if men should constitute themselves his enemies, he will regard them kindly, understanding their ignorance, and making full allowance for it. When this state of heart is arrived at, then is the third step in the discipline of one's self-seeking inclinations accomplished; then is the third great lesson in Virtue and Knowledge learned and mastered.

Having thus laid down the first ten steps and three lessons in right-doing and right-knowing, I leave those of my readers who are prepared for them to learn and master them in their everyday life. There is, of course, a still higher discipline of the body, a more far-reaching discipline of the tongue, and greater and more all-embracing virtues to acquire and understand before the highest state of bliss and knowledge can be apprehended, but it is not my purpose to deal with them here. I have expounded only the first and easiest lessons on the Higher Path, and by the time these are thoroughly mastered, the reader will have become so purified, strengthened, and enlightened, that he will not be left in the dark as to his future progress. Those of my readers who have completed these three lessons will already have perceived, beyond and above, the high altitudes of Truth, and the narrow and precipitous track which leads to them, and will choose whether they shall proceed.

The straight Path which I have laid down can be pursued by all with greater profit to themselves and to the world, and even those who do not aspire to the attainment of Truth, will develop greater intellectual and moral strength, finer judgment, and deeper peace of mind by perfecting themselves in this Path. Nor will their material prosperity suffer by this change of heart; nay, it will be rendered truer, purer, and more enduring, for if there is one who is capable of succeeding and fitted to achieve, it is the man who has abandoned the petty dissipations[8] and everyday vices of his kind, who is strong to rule his body and his mind, and who pursues with fixed resolve the path of unswerving integrity and sterling virtue.

---

[8] Careless, useless, and profitless activities.

Mental Conditions & Their Effects

Without going into the details of the greater steps and lessons in the right life (a task outside the scope of this small work), a few hints and statements concerning those mental conditions from which life in its totality springs will prove helpful to those who are ready and willing to penetrate further into that inner realm of heart and mind where Love and Wisdom and Peace await the strenuous comer.

All sin is ignorance. It is a condition of darkness and undevelopment. The wrong-thinker and wrong-doer is in the same position in the school of life as is the ignorant pupil in the school of learning. He has yet to learn how to think and act correctly, that is, in accordance with Law. The pupil in learning is not happy so long as he does his lessons wrongly, and unhappiness cannot be escaped while sin remains unconquered.

Life is a series of lessons. Some are diligent in learning them, and they become pure, wise, and altogether happy. Others are negligent, and do not apply themselves, and they remain impure, foolish, and unhappy.

Every form of unhappiness springs from a wrong

condition of mind. Happiness inheres in right conditions of mind. Happiness is mental harmony; unhappiness is mental inharmony. While a man lives in wrong conditions of mind, he will live a wrong life, and will suffer continually. Suffering is rooted in error. Bliss inheres in enlightenment. There is salvation for man only in the destruction of his own ignorance, error, and self-delusion. Where there are wrong conditions of mind there is bondage and unrest; where there are right conditions of mind there is freedom and peace.

Here are some of the leading wrong mental conditions and their disastrous effects upon the life:

Wrong Mental Conditions	Their Effects
Hatred	Injury, violence, disaster, and suffering.
Lust	Confusion of intellect, remorse, shame, and wretchedness.
Covetousness	Fear, unrest, unhappiness, and loss.
Pride	Disappointment, chagrin, lack of self-knowledge.
Vanity	Distress, and mortification of spirit.
Condemnation	Persecution, hatred from others.
Ill-will	Failures and troubles.
Self-indulgence	Misery, loss of judgment, grossness, disease, and neglect.
Anger	Loss of power and influence.
Desire, or Self-slavery	Grief, folly, sorrow, uncertainty, and loneliness.

Mental Conditions & Their Effects

The above wrong conditions of mind are merely negations; they are states of darkness and deprivation and not of positive power. Evil is not a power; it is *ignorance and misuse of good*. The hater is he who has failed to do the lesson of Love correctly, and he suffers in consequence. When he succeeds in doing it rightly, the hatred will have disappeared, and he will see and understand the darkness and impotence of hatred. It is so with every wrong condition.

The following are some of the more important right mental conditions and their beneficent effects upon the life:

Right Mental Conditions	Their Effects
Love	Gentle conditions, bliss, and blessedness.
Purity	Intellectual clearness, joy, invincible confidence.
Selflessness	Courage, satisfaction, happiness, and plenty.
Humility	Calmness, restfulness, knowledge of Truth.
Meekness	Equipoise, contentment under all circumstances.
Compassion	Protection, love and reverence from others.
Goodwill	Gladness and success.
Self-control	Peace of mind, true judgment, refinement, health, and honor.
Patience	Mental power, far-reaching influence.
Self-conquest	Enlightenment, wisdom, insight, and profound peace.

The above right conditions of mind are states of positive power, of light, of joyful possession, and of knowledge. The good man *knows*. He has learned to do his lessons correctly, and thereby understands the exact proportions which make up the sum of life. He is enlightened, and knows good and evil. He is supremely happy, doing only that which is divinely right.

The man who is involved in the wrong conditions of mind, does not know. He is ignorant of good and evil, of himself, of the inward causes which make his life. He is unhappy, and believes other people are entirely the cause of his unhappiness. He works blindly, and lives in darkness, seeing no central purpose in existence, and no orderly and lawful sequence in the course of things.

He who aspires to the attainment of the Higher Life in its completion — who would perceive with unveiled vision the true order of things and the meaning of life — let him abandon all the wrong conditions of heart, and persevere unceasingly in the practice of the good. If he suffers, or doubts, or is unhappy, let him search within until he finds the cause, and having found it, let him cast it away. Let him so guard and purify his heart that every day less of evil and more of good shall issue therefrom; so will he daily become stronger, nobler, wiser; so will his blessedness increase, and the Light of Truth, growing ever brighter and brighter within him, will dispel all gloom, and illuminate his Pathway.

Exhortation

Disciples of Truth, lovers of Virtue, seekers of Wisdom; ye, also, who are sorrow-stricken, knowing the emptiness of the self-life, and who aspire to the life that is supremely beautiful, and serenely glad — take now yourselves in hand, enter the Door of Discipline, and know the Better Life.

Put away self-delusion; behold yourself as you are, and see the Path of Virtue as it is. There is no lazy way to Truth. He who would stand upon the mountain's summit must strenuously climb, and must rest only to gather strength. But if the climbing is less glorious than the cloudless summit, it is still glorious. Discipline in itself is beautiful, and the end of discipline is sweet.

Rise early and meditate. Begin each day with a conquered body, and a mind fortified against error and weakness. Temptation will never be overcome by unprepared fighting. The mind must be armed and arrayed in the silent hour. It must be trained to perceive, to know, to understand. Sin and temptation disappear when right understanding is developed.

Right understanding is reached through unabated

discipline. Truth cannot be reached but through discipline. Patience will increase by effort and practice, and patience will make discipline beautiful.

Discipline is irksome to the impatient man and the self-lover, so he avoids it, and continues to live loosely and confusedly.

Discipline is not irksome to the Truth-lover, and he will find the infinite patience which can wait and work and overcome. As the joy of the gardener who sees his flowers develop day by day, so is the joy of the man of discipline who sees the divine flowers of Purity, Wisdom, Compassion, and Love grow up in his heart.

The loose-liver cannot escape sorrow and pain. The undisciplined mind falls, weak and helpless, before the fierce onslaught of passion.

Array well your mind, then, lover of Truth. Be watchful, thoughtful, resolute. Your salvation is at hand; your readiness and effort are all that are needed. If you should fail ten times, do not be disheartened; if you should fail a hundred times, rise up and pursue your way; if you should fail a thousand times, do not despair. When the right Path is entered, success is sure if the Path is not utterly abandoned.

First strife, and then victory. First labor, and then rest. First weakness, and then strength. In the beginning the lower life, and the glare and confusion of battle, and at the end the Life Beautiful, the Silence, and the Peace.

James Allen:
A Prophet of Meditation

Although the late James Allen, of Ilfracombe, is comparatively unknown, yet to thousands of seekers after truth, he has proved a guide, philosopher, and friend. One of his works, *As a Man Thinketh*, has gone into no less than eleven editions; surely proof that he has a considerable vogue. The most casual reader of any of his works cannot fail to be impressed by the simplicity, cheerfulness, and benevolence which seem to radiate from the soul of the writer. We cannot place James Allen in any exclusive category, as he teaches so much that harmonizes with all the best thought of our age. Liberal Christians, Theosophists,[1] and many other enlightened bodies of truth-seekers may claim him as an exponent of at least several of their distinctive views; but he was simply a strong, true, individual man who wrote and spoke out of the depth of his own convictions, and never held himself bound to voice the peculiar tenets of any cult. Wide

---

[1] Members of any of a number of philosophies maintaining that a knowledge of God may be achieved through spiritual ecstasy, direct intuition, or special individual relations, especially the movement founded in 1875 as the Theosophical Society by Helena Blavatsky (1831–1891) and Henry Steel Olcott (1832–1907).

knowledge of the Scriptures of the world, professedly sacred and other, coupled with intense sympathy with all human causes have rendered his works a delight to the scholar, as well as an inspiration to the less cultured aspirant for instruction in that path of wisdom which inevitably leads to power and peace. His literary style is clear and simple, and in dealing with subjects that are often vague and illusory, he used language that made his meaning easily understood. James Allen disliked publicity, and, perhaps, it is because of his disregard of the uses of advertisement that he is not so well known as he might otherwise have been. After all, however, it is the man's message that matters, and he who runs[2] may read in the James Allen Library the story of the spiritual life of the writer. The worship of the personality was a thing that he always guarded against, and for that reason his body was cremated and his ashes scattered to the four winds of Heaven,[3] so that no man or woman in the future could make a place of pilgrimage of his grave, or say "the dust of James Allen lies here." His books alone are monuments to his memory, and they are being sent with the utmost speed to all the corners of the earth, and are being translated into various languages. *The Eight Pillars of Prosperity* (1911) has just been published in the Spanish tongue.

James Allen was born in Leicester[4] on November 28th, 1864. His father was at one time a very prosperous manufacturer, but evil days overtook him when James

---

[2] In this context, grows and develops.
[3] A poetic and symbolic expression found in various religious and literary texts (most notably the Bible), generally referring to the four cardinal directions—North, East, South, and West—symbolizing completeness, universality, or the entirety of the earth.
[4] The county town of Leicestershire and largest city in the East Midlands of England.

A Prophet of Meditation

was about fifteen years of age. Nearly everything was lost, and Allen, senior, taking what money was left, went to America to make a new home for his wife and family, but within two days of his arrival in that country he met with an accident and died in a New York hospital. His empty pocketbook and an old silver watch were returned to the family as the only things found upon him. James now found himself in his native town of Leicester, at the age of fifteen, with a mother and two younger brothers to support. He worked as many as fifteen hours a day in a factory, but never gave up his beloved books.

Mrs. Allen states that at the age of seventeen, he found his father's Shakespeare, of which he became an ardent reader. "I read Shakespeare," he himself has said, "in the early morning, at breakfast time, in the dinner hour, and in the evening." He knew the whole of the plays by heart ultimately, and could lose himself in them when surrounded by hundreds of workmen and by the whir and thud of machinery.

Then came Emerson's[5] *Essays*,[6] calm and radiant, revealing to him a higher realm than that of the passions with their fleeting pleasures and certain pains. "Circles," "Compensation," "The Over-Soul," and "Self-Reliance" were the essays which impressed him most,[7] particularly "Self-Reliance," which showed him the importance of conduct and the worth and dignity of character. It helped him to battle successfully with a natural timidity, which put a check on initiative and originality.

Then, at the age of 24, he came across Sir Edwin

---

[5] Ralph Waldo Emerson (1803–1882) was an American lecturer, philosopher, abolitionist, and poet who led the transcendentalist movement of the mid-19th century.

[6] Several of Emerson's essays were collected in a *First Series* (1841) and *Second Series* (1844).

[7] All can be found in Emerson's *Essays: First Series* (1841).

Arnold's[8] *The Light of Asia*. Describing his sensations on reading it, he has said, "I could not stir from my seat till I read every word. When I did rise from the reading of this book, it was as though I had become a different man. A curtain seemed to have rolled back from the face of the Universe, and I saw the causes and meaning of things which had hitherto been dark mysteries. There was a revelation which was almost blending in its brilliance and suddenness, an exaltation which alarmed me while it transported me into a felicitous[9] insight. The vision quickly faded, but its influence remained, the memory of it saving me in many an hour of darkness and temptation, until that calmer time of meditation and knowledge, ten years later, when it returned never again to fade from the mind." In *The Light of Asia*,[10] Sir Edwin Arnold sought, by the medium of an imaginary Buddhist votary,[11] to depict the life and character and indicate the philosophy of that noble hero and reformer, Prince Gautama of India, the founder of Buddhism. "More than a third of mankind owe their moral and religious ideas to this illustrious prince, whose personality, though imperfectly revealed in the existing sources of information, cannot but appear the highest, gentlest, holiest, and most beneficent, with one exception, in the history of Thought."

> If ye lay bound upon the wheel of change,
>   And no way were of breaking from the chain,
>   The Heart of boundless Being is a curse,
>   The Soul of Things fell Pain.

---

[8] Sir Edwin Arnold (1832–1904) was an English poet and journalist.
[9] Pleasant and fortunate.
[10] Published in London in July 1879, the book, in the form of a narrative poem, describes the life of Prince Gautama Buddha, who, after attaining enlightenment, became Buddha, The Awakened One.
[11] One devoted, consecrated, or engaged by vow or promise.

A Prophet of Meditation

Ye are not bound! the Soul of Things is sweet,
    The Heart of Being is celestial rest;
Stronger than woe is will; that which was Good
    Doth pass to Better—Best.

I, Buddha, who wept with all my brother's tears,
    Whose heart was broken by a whole world's woe,
Laugh and am glad, for there is Liberty!
    Ho! ye who suffer! know

Ye suffer from yourselves. None else compels,
    None other holds you that ye live and die,
And whirl upon the wheel, and hug and kiss
    Its spokes of agony,

Its tire of tears, its nave of nothingness.
    Behold, I show you Truth! Lower than hell,
Higher than heaven, outside the utmost stars,
    Farther than Brahm doth dwell,

Before beginning, and without an end,
    As space eternal and as surety sure,
Is fixed a Power divine which moves to good,
    Only its laws endure.[12]

From the date of reading *The Light of Asia* began James Allen's great search for truth.

At the age of 26 came *The Bhagavad Gita*.[13] There followed the books of the Chinese sages and *The Gospel of Buddha* (1894) by Paul Carus,[14] Dr. Bucke's[15] *Cosmic*

---

[12] An excerpt from "Book The Eighth" of *The Light of Asia*.
[13] A Hindu religious text dated to the second or first century BC.
[14] Paul Carus (1852–1919) was a German-American author, editor, philosopher, and a student of comparative religion.
[15] Richard Maurice Bucke (1837–1902) was a Canadian psychiatrist.

Consciousness[16] also had an influence on him, inasmuch as it gave a scientific explanation of what had already been revealed inwardly.

When about the age of 25, James Allen left his native town and went to London, where he was for a time a private secretary, working from 9 to 6 o'clock, and using every moment out of office hours for writing his books. He afterward founded *The Light of Reason*, and gave up his time to the work of editing the magazine, at the same time carrying on a voluminous correspondence with searchers after truth all over the world. He met Mrs. Allen, who was a sister in an East End mission at the time, when he was 29 years of age.[17] She proved a true mate, and now carries on the work which her husband inaugurated. Leaving London, they took up residence in beautiful Ilfracombe, where the remainder of James Allen's life was spent. His first book was *From Poverty to Power* (1901), which is considered to be his best work. It has passed into many editions, and Mrs. Allen states that tens of thousands have been sold all over the world, both authorized and pirated editions. In this book he urges the reader to strive to realize, and not merely hold as a theory, that evil is a passing phase, a self-created shadow; that all your pains, sorrows, and misfortunes have come to you by a process of undeviating and absolutely perfect law; have come to you because you deserve and require them,

---

[16] *Cosmic Consciousness: A Study in the Evolution of the Human Mind* (1901) explores the concept of consciousness, wherein Bucke discerns three forms, or degrees, of consciousness: Simple consciousness, possessed by both animals and mankind; Self-consciousness, possessed by mankind, encompassing thought, reason, and imagination; Cosmic consciousness, which is "a higher form of consciousness than that possessed by the ordinary man."

[17] Lily L. Allen (née Oram, 1867–1952) was an Irish author. In her twenties, she joined the Bible Christian Church and for a time was known as Sister Lily. While conducting a mission in South Wales, she met James and they were married in May 1895.

A Prophet of Meditation

and that by first enduring, and then understanding them, you may be made stronger, wiser, nobler. He says: "When you have fully entered into this realization, you will be in a position to mold your own circumstances, to transmute all evil into good, and to weave, with a master hand, the fabric of your destiny." Soon after the publication of *From Poverty to Power* came *All These Things Added* (1903), and then, *As a Man Thinketh* (1903). Other books followed, such as *Through the Gate of Good* (1903), *Byways of Blessedness* (1904), *Out from the Heart* (1904), *The Life Triumphant* (1908), *The Mastery of Destiny* (1909), *Above Life's Turmoil* (1910), *From Passion to Peace* (1910), *The Eight Pillars of Prosperity* (1911), and *Man: King of Mind, Body, and Circumstance* (1911). James Allen took a keen interest in many scientific subjects, delighting in astronomy, geology, and botany, and might have written on a wide range of subjects had he chosen to do so. He was often asked for articles on many questions outside his own particular work, but he refused to comply, concentrating his whole thought and effort on preaching the gospel of selflessness. After a short illness, he died on January 24th, 1912,[18] in the forty-eighth year of his age. Six days later his remains were cremated at Leicester, and his ashes were devoutly scattered to the four winds with the following invocation, uttered audibly:

> "As these ashes of James Allen are cast to the four winds of heaven, so may the truth he taught permeate to the four corners of the earth, carrying with it joy, peace, and consolation."

Although what James Allen taught may not be new — old truth in a new setting — yet the direct and forceful

---

[18] From tuberculosis.

style in which he expressed his thoughts undoubtedly give him a special niche among ethical writers. His magazine, *The Light of Reason*, was founded in 1902. It took hold of a large number of the thinking public at once, and its usefulness was assured. Immediately upon its publication, letters began to pour in from all parts of the kingdom,[19] from all sorts and conditions of men and women asking for advice, for spiritual help and guidance. Later, when the magazine found its way to America, Australia, New Zealand, India, and the Far East, the correspondence became so heavy that for hours every day Mr. Allen did nothing but answer letters.

In 1905, he established The Brotherhood, or School of Virtue, the central doctrine of which is the renunciation of self for the good of the world, and necessarily its corollary,[20] the practice of divine love toward all creatures and beings. The rules of the Brotherhood are those principles of truth which the seekers after righteousness in all ages have adopted. Religions change from age to age, but the principles of divine virtue are eternally the same, and these principles are embodied in the rules of the Brotherhood. In June 1910, *The Epoch* was started. With it is incorporated *The Light of Reason*. It is edited by Mrs. Allen, and has a large and increasing sale in all parts of the world.

I have called James Allen a prophet of meditation, because meditation was one of the chief things he emphasized in his writings. He always urged that each man must learn the truth for himself. Reading books and accepting what is said as you may accept the food that is put before you is not enough. He points out in his book,

---
[19] Meaning the U.K. (United Kingdom).
[20] A direct, practical, or natural consequence, effect, or result.

The Mastery of Destiny, that aspiration must be united to concentration, the result being meditation. When a man intensely desires to reach and realize a higher, purer, and more radiant life than the merely worldly and pleasure-loving life, he engages in aspiration, and when he earnestly concentrates his thoughts upon the finding of that life, he practices meditation.

Without intense aspiration, there can be no meditation. The more intense the nature of a man, the more readily will he find meditation, and the more successfully will he practice it. The meditative life is a child of the East, and though both preached and practiced by the Master, it is made conspicuous today by its absence from the habit of the great majority of religious people. The men who have had most influence in the world have been the spiritually developed men, and, therefore, spiritual development ought to be our chief aim. Spiritual development can only be obtained by meditation, which consists in bringing the mind to a focus in its search for the Divine knowledge, the Divine life; the intense dwelling in thought on Truth. The object of meditation is Divine enlightenment, the attainment of truth, and is, therefore, interwoven with practical purity and righteousness. Thus, while at first the time spent in actual meditation is short — perhaps only half-an-hour in the early morning — the knowledge gained in that half-hour of vivid aspiration and concentrated thought is embodied in practice during the whole day. In meditation, therefore, the entire life of a man is involved; and as he advances in practice he becomes more and more fitted to perform the duties of life in the circumstances in which he may be placed, for he becomes stronger, holier, calmer, and wiser.

Many people think they are meditating when they

are simply indulging in reverie or a brown study.[21] This is a fatal error. James Allen points out that reverie is a loose dreaming into which a man falls: meditation is a strong, purposeful thinking to which a man rises. Reverie is easy and pleasurable; meditation is at first difficult and irksome. Reverie thrives in indolence and luxury: meditation arises from strenuousness and discipline. Reverie is first alluring, then sensuous, and then sensual. Meditation is first forbidding, then profitable, and then peaceful. Reverie is dangerous, it undermines self-control. Meditation is protective, it establishes self-control.

Now, James Allen shows that there are certain signs by which one can know whether he is engaging in reverie or meditation, and I think these will prove of interest. The indications of reverie are: A desire to avoid exertion; a desire to experience the pleasure of dreaming; an increasing distaste for one's worldly duties; a desire to shirk one's worldly responsibilities; fear of consequences; a wish to get money with as little effort as possible; lack of self-control.

The indications of meditation are: Increase of both physical and mental energy; a strenuous striving after wisdom; a decrease of irksomeness in the performance of duty; a fixed determination to fulfill faithfully all worldly responsibilities; freedom from fear; indifference to riches; possession of self-control.

Of course, meditation is not possible under certain circumstances. The times, places, and conditions in which James Allen considered meditation impossible are as follow: At, or immediately after, meals; in places of pleasure; in crowded places; while walking rapidly; while lying in bed in the morning; while smoking.

---

[21] A brown study is a state of being so absorbed in thought that you become unaware of your surroundings.

A Prophet of Meditation

Here is a list of the times, places, and conditions in which meditation is difficult: At night; in a luxuriously furnished room; while sitting on a soft, yielding seat; while wearing gay apparel; when in company; when the body is weary; if the body is given too much food.

The times, places, and conditions in which it is best to meditate are: Very early in the morning; immediately before meals; in solitude; in the open air, or in a plainly furnished room; while sitting on a hard seat; when the body is strong and vigorous; when the body is modestly and plainly clothed.

The difficulty, of course, with the beginner is how to set about the practice of meditation. He may get up in the morning to meditate, but presently his mind drifts on to one thing and another. Aspiration can often best be aroused and the mind renewed in meditation by the mental repetition of a lofty precept, a beautiful sentence, or a verse of poetry. Indeed, the mind that is ready for meditation will instinctively adopt this practice.

> Murdo S. Carruthers[22]
> *Herald of the Star*[23]
> March 1916

---

[22] Murdo Stewart Carruthers (1879–1917) was an editor and Lance Corporal of the Argyll and Sutherland Highlanders. In 1917, at the time of his death by sniper during World War I, he was attached to the 6th Battalion Cameron Highlanders.

[23] The official publication of the Order of the Star in the East (OSE), an international organization established by the Theosophical Society. The first issue appeared in January 1912 and ran until it became the *International Star Bulletin* in January 1928.

"Men do not attract that which they *want*, but that which they *are*."

www.ingramcontent.com/pod-product-compliance
Lightning Source LLC
Chambersburg PA
CBHW060535080526
44586CB00012B/739